OPPOSING VIEWPOINTS® SERIES

Advertising

Other Books of Related Interest:

Opposing Viewpoints Series
The Culture of Beauty

At Issue Series
How Does Advertising Impact Teen Behavior?

Current Controversies Series
Capitalism

"Congress shall make no law . . . abridging the freedom of speech, or of the press."

First Amendment to the U.S. Constitution

The basic foundation of our democracy is the First Amendment guarantee of freedom of expression. The Opposing Viewpoints Series is dedicated to the concept of this basic freedom and the idea that it is more important to practice it than to enshrine it.

OPPOSING VIEWPOINTS® SERIES

Advertising

Roman Espejo, Book Editor

GREENHAVEN PRESS
A part of Gale, Cengage Learning

GALE
CENGAGE Learning™

Detroit • New York • San Francisco • New Haven, Conn • Waterville, Maine • London

26.75

Christine Nasso, *Publisher*
Elizabeth Des Chenes, *Managing Editor*

© 2010 Greenhaven Press, a part of Gale, Cengage Learning.

Gale and Greenhaven Press are registered trademarks used herein under license.

For more information, contact:
Greenhaven Press
27500 Drake Rd.
Farmington Hills, MI 48331-3535
Or you can visit our Internet site at gale.cengage.com

For product information and technology assistance, contact us at

Gale Customer Support, 1-800-877-4253
For permission to use material from this text or product, submit all requests online at www.cengage.com/permissions

Further permissions questions can be emailed to permissionrequest@cengage.com

Articles in Greenhaven Press anthologies are often edited for length to meet page requirements. In addition, original titles of these works are changed to clearly present the main thesis and to explicitly indicate the author's opinion. Every effort is made to ensure that Greenhaven Press accurately reflects the original intent of the authors. Every effort has been made to trace the owners of copyrighted material.

Cover Image copyright Oculo, 2010. Used under license from Shutterstock.com.

LIBRARY OF CONGRESS CATALOGING-IN-PUBLICATION DATA

Advertising / Roman Espejo, book editor.
    p. cm. -- (Opposing viewpoints)
  Includes bibliographical references and index.
  ISBN 978-0-7377-4751-5 (hardcover) -- ISBN 978-0-7377-4752-2 (pbk.)
  1. Advertising--Moral and ethical aspects--Juvenile literature. 2. Advertising--Social aspects--Juvenile literature. I. Espejo, Roman, 1977-
  HF5831.A342 2010
  659.1--dc22

                                             2009050761

Printed in the United States of America
1 2 3 4 5 6 7 14 13 12 11 10

Contents

Why Consider Opposing Viewpoints?

> *"The only way in which a human being can make some approach to knowing the whole of a subject is by hearing what can be said about it by persons of every variety of opinion and studying all modes in which it can be looked at by every character of mind. No wise man ever acquired his wisdom in any mode but this."*
>
> *John Stuart Mill*

In our media-intensive culture it is not difficult to find differing opinions. Thousands of newspapers and magazines and dozens of radio and television talk shows resound with differing points of view. The difficulty lies in deciding which opinion to agree with and which "experts" seem the most credible. The more inundated we become with differing opinions and claims, the more essential it is to hone critical reading and thinking skills to evaluate these ideas. Opposing Viewpoints books address this problem directly by presenting stimulating debates that can be used to enhance and teach these skills. The varied opinions contained in each book examine many different aspects of a single issue. While examining these conveniently edited opposing views, readers can develop critical thinking skills such as the ability to compare and contrast authors' credibility, facts, argumentation styles, use of persuasive techniques, and other stylistic tools. In short, the Opposing Viewpoints Series is an ideal way to attain the higher-level thinking and reading skills so essential in a culture of diverse and contradictory opinions.

In addition to providing a tool for critical thinking, Opposing Viewpoints books challenge readers to question their own strongly held opinions and assumptions. Most people form their opinions on the basis of upbringing, peer pressure, and personal, cultural, or professional bias. By reading carefully balanced opposing views, readers must directly confront new ideas as well as the opinions of those with whom they disagree. This is not to simplistically argue that everyone who reads opposing views will—or should—change his or her opinion. Instead, the series enhances readers' understanding of their own views by encouraging confrontation with opposing ideas. Careful examination of others' views can lead to the readers' understanding of the logical inconsistencies in their own opinions, perspective on why they hold an opinion, and the consideration of the possibility that their opinion requires further evaluation.

Evaluating Other Opinions

To ensure that this type of examination occurs, Opposing Viewpoints books present all types of opinions. Prominent spokespeople on different sides of each issue as well as well-known professionals from many disciplines challenge the reader. An additional goal of the series is to provide a forum for other, less known, or even unpopular viewpoints. The opinion of an ordinary person who has had to make the decision to cut off life support from a terminally ill relative, for example, may be just as valuable and provide just as much insight as a medical ethicist's professional opinion. The editors have two additional purposes in including these less known views. One, the editors encourage readers to respect others' opinions—even when not enhanced by professional credibility. It is only by reading or listening to and objectively evaluating others' ideas that one can determine whether they are worthy of consideration. Two, the inclusion of such viewpoints encourages the important critical thinking skill of objectively evaluating an author's credentials and bias. This evaluation will illuminate an author's reasons for taking a particular stance on an issue and will aid in readers' evaluation of the author's ideas.

It is our hope that these books will give readers a deeper understanding of the issues debated and an appreciation of the complexity of even seemingly simple issues when good and honest people disagree. This awareness is particularly important in a democratic society such as ours in which people enter into public debate to determine the common good. Those with whom one disagrees should not be regarded as enemies but rather as people whose views deserve careful examination and may shed light on one's own.

Thomas Jefferson once said that "difference of opinion leads to inquiry, and inquiry to truth." Jefferson, a broadly educated man, argued that "if a nation expects to be ignorant and free . . . it expects what never was and never will be." As individuals and as a nation, it is imperative that we consider the opinions of others and examine them with skill and discernment. The Opposing Viewpoints Series is intended to help readers achieve this goal.

David L. Bender and Bruno Leone,
Founders

Introduction

> *"A world without advertising is less far-fetched than you think, at least when it comes to outdoor."*
>
> —*Claudia Penteado
> and Andrew Hampp*[1]

On January 7, 2009, the billboard ban in the city of Los Angeles, California, was upheld by the U.S. Court of Appeals for the Ninth Circuit. The court ruled that the 2002 prohibition on outdoor advertising did not infringe on the free speech rights of Metro Lights LLC, a sign company, and overturned a lower court judgment. Metro Lights contended that if the city sold space for ads on booths and bus benches, it cannot restrict additional off-site signs. "It's certainly a significant ruling, and it is a blow to the outdoor advertising industry,"[2] stated Paul E. Fischer, attorney for Metro Lights. He continued that the federal ruling could impact municipal billboard laws in other states. In contrast, councilman Bill Rosenthal supported the decision. "Obviously, we have seen billboards pop up like mushrooms in our district," he claimed. "It has been totally out of control."[3] An estimated four thousand unapproved billboards have been erected in Los Angeles.

Cindy Miscikowski, a councilwoman from 1995 to 2005, was behind the ban and a longtime advocate against billboards in the city. "The ordinance I authored is pretty straightforward," she said. "It states that billboards are not to be built in Los Angeles. The only caveat to that would be that they will be allowed to be erected in areas where a specific plan or supplemental use district has been enacted."[4] Skeptics, however, assert that so-called "sign districts" are actually loopholes for outdoor advertising. In March 2009, activists rallied against the designation of twenty-one sign districts in Los Angeles, fearing that digital billboards and "supergraphics"—huge plastic or vinyl signs hung or fitted on buildings—would proliferate in these areas. For example, Patricia Barragan claimed a supergraphic that covered the Santa Monica Boulevard building where she rents an office disrupted her physical therapy practice. "The first patients who came in at 7 o'clock said, 'What is this? This is depressing. I don't want to be treated in these depressing rooms.'"[5] Barragan also said that the two-story ad blocked windows and darkened her treatment room by 40 percent.

The movement against billboards caught worldwide attention when the city of São Paolo, Brazil, decided to eliminate nearly all outdoor ads—thirteen thousand of them—starting in 2007. Proponents of the "Clean City" ordinance declared it would cut down on "visual pollution"—not only billboards, but also fliers and the size of store displays. "I know the bill is radical, but it's emblematic," stated mayor Gilberto Kassab. "It's controversial, but necessary for the city."[6] Roberto Pompeu de Toledo, a Brazilian columnist and author, called its passage "a rare victory of the public interest over private, of order over disorder, aesthetics over ugliness, of cleanliness over trash."[7]

Opponents lamented the bill, speculating that it would rob gritty São Paolo of character and vibrancy. "It would be like New York without Times Square,"[8] insisted one resident. Some advertisers in the city viewed the ordinance as an economic choke hold. "This is a radical law that damages the rules of a market economy and respect for the rule of law," argued Marcel Solimeo of the Commercial Association of São Paulo. "We live in a consumer society and the essence of capitalism is the availability of information about products."[9]

In the United States, Alaska, Hawaii, Maine, and Vermont currently outlaw billboards. Kevin Fry, president of Scenic America, believes that remaining states may not follow in their footsteps. "The state legislatures have been completely captured by the billboard industry,"[10] says Fry. No Ad Here, an activist Web site, proposes that consumers and policy makers take action: "It's time to boycott products and services . . . [that] clutter our lives with this intrusive junk. It's time to pass legislation to really reduce the number and size of billboards."[11]

Still, not all Americans take a negative stance on billboards. In a letter to the editor in the *New York Times*, Larry Penner of Great Neck, New York, defended them and criticized antibillboard groups. "How ironic that those who defend public displays of artwork that some might consider pornographic are so quick to censor outdoor advertisers," he wrote. "There are many small business and building owners who struggle to survive because of excessive government regulations, property taxes, and rent control."[12]

The billboard is just one hot button topic in advertising. *Opposing Viewpoints: Advertising* presents some of the varied and conflicting positions on advertising and marketing in the following chapters: Is Advertising Harmful? Does Advertising Exploit Children? Should Political Advertising Be Reformed? and What Is the Future of Advertising? From corporate sponsorships in schools to campaigns for social causes, the ad industry and its modes of communication and branding court controversy and inquiry.

Notes

1. *Advertising Age*, October 1, 2007.
2. *Los Angeles Times*, January 7, 2007. www.latimes.com.
3. *Los Angeles Times*, January 7, 2007. www.latimes.com.
4. Coalition to Ban Billboard Blight, May 2002. http://banbillboardblight.org.
5. *Los Angeles Times*, January 20, 2009. www.latimes.com.
6. BBC, September 19, 2006. http://news.bbc.co.uk.
7. *New York Times*, December 12, 2006. www.nytimes.com.

8. BBC, September 19, 2006. http://news.bbc.co.uk.

9. *New York Times*, December 12, 2006. www.nytimes.com.

10. *Portland Press Herald*, July 29, 2007. http://pressherald .mainetoday.com.

11. No Ad Here. www.noadhere.org.

12. *New York Times*, February 18, 2007. www.nytimes.com.

Is Advertising Harmful?

Chapter Preface

In 2008, men's lifestyle Web site AskMen.com ranked what it considered to be the ten worst "male-bashing ads." It singled out commercials from Pizza Hut to AT&T to Sony for depicting men as clueless, unable to fend for themselves, and even the inferior sex in relationships. "The clichéd message is that women are the civilized voice burdened with managing men and their ingrained frat-boy mind-set,"[1] argues Marc Voyer, an entertainment correspondent. Moreover, he claims that a survey conducted by Children Now, a public policy organization, shows that youngsters perceived men on television as corrupt by a margin of seventeen to one.

Tom Nakayama, professor and chair of the Department of Communication Studies at Northeastern University, alleges that subtler male stereotypes can still be powerful. "With their images of cowboys, successful businessmen, construction workers, sophisticates in tuxedos, muscle men, and others, advertisements may seem to be flashing by casually. But they actually represent countless—if often unconscious—decisions by writers, advertisers, producers, programmers, and others about what men look like, say, and even think." Nakayama suggests this ties manhood to little else but aggression, domination, and a lack of emotion. "Advertising narrows the definition of what it means to be a man,"[2] he claims.

Nonetheless, others contend that sexist advertisements are part of the larger problem of the industry. "Advertising is not sexist. It's not racist. It's not homophobic," asserts Kevin Gamble, a Salon.com commentator. "To label it in ways that apply only to one group is to miss the bigger picture that endangers us all—the blindly inhuman nature of this media manipulation."[3] In the following chapter, the authors deliberate whether advertising harms or enriches society.

Notes

1. AskMen.com. www.askmen.com.
2. Media & Values, Fall 1989. www.medialit.org/media_values .html.
3. Salon.com, November 10, 2008. www.salon.com.

| "If consumers did not benefit from advertising, it would not work."

Advertising Benefits Consumers

Winston Fletcher

In the following viewpoint, Winston Fletcher argues that critics of advertising focus on specific types of advertisements—alcohol, junk food, and credit cards, for example—without examining the benefits of advertising as a whole. Fletcher asserts that advertising supports the economy and subsidizes the media, keeping them low cost and free from many forms of state control. He alleges that advertising enables sellers and the public to communicate, increasing consumer awareness and choice. Fletcher is the chair of the Advertising Standards Board of Finance in London and author of Powers of Persuasion: The Inside Story of British Advertising.

As you read, consider the following questions:

1. As stated by Winston Fletcher, what are the public's views of advertising in Great Britain?

2. According to Fletcher, how does Raymond Williams take the argument against advertising further?

Winston Fletcher, "Art or Puffery? A Defence of Advertising," *New Humanist*, June 2008. Reproduced by permission.

3. How does the author respond to the allegation that advertising emphasizes emotional and sexual desires?

At end of the 20th century British advertising creativity ruled the world. Brilliant campaigns—like those for Smash instant mashed potato (Martians); Heineken beer ('Refreshes the Parts Other Beers Cannot Reach'); Benson & Hedges cigarettes (Surrealist Posters); Levi's jeans ('Launderette'); the Health Education Council (Pregnant Man); John Smith's Bitter (Arkwright); Hovis bread (Boy on a Bike); Carlsberg beer (Dam Busters) and a galaxy of others garnered garlands galore at international creative festivals. In 1978 in Cannes, for example, Britain won the Grand Prix for both television and cinema—a rare occurrence—and snitched a massive 80 Gold, Silver and Bronze Lions.

But none of this cut much ice with advertising's enemies back home. In the 1970s the advertising trade paper *Campaign* invited 21 influential opinion leaders to publish essays titled 'What I Think About Advertising'. The list included leftist Labour MP [member of Parliament] Christopher Mayhew, economists Sir Roy Harrod and Joan Robinson, moral crusader Mary Whitehouse, television dramatist Ted Willis, academics John Cohen and Raymond Williams, and a newsroom full of top journalists including Richard Clements, Richard Ingrams, Brian Inglis, Peter Jenkins, Jill Tweedie and Peregrine Worsthorne. The series provoked outrage in the admen's favourite watering holes, from Soho pubs to St. James's clubs.

A Fair Slice of Intellectual Opinion

Nobody pretended the 21 were representative of the population at large. But they represented a fair slice of then current British intellectual opinion. And few of them liked advertising one iota. Twelve were extremely hostile, four were mildly hostile, four saw a few pros buried among countless cons—but only Peregrine Worsthorne was broadly enthusiastic about the contribution advertising makes to society.

The criticism ranged from a fundamental disapproval of advertising as a phenomenon, to individual dislikes of certain of its characteristics. Christopher Mayhew contended that advertising had a wholly corrupting effect on society. Mary Whitehouse said it degraded women. *Tribune* editor Richard Clements believed it to be economically wasteful (echoing the views of the then prime minister Harold Wilson). Many of the 21 insisted advertising encourages materialism. Christopher Mayhew—who in the 1950s had fought the launch of commercial television tooth and nail, supported by Tory as well as Labour leaders—argued:

> "'Advertising introduces you to the good things of life.' Such was the slogan plugged by the Advertising Association a few years ago. That is to say, the good things of life, according to the Advertising Association, are the things we see advertised, the things we can buy—not honesty, friendship, kindness or good manners; not loyalty, respect for law or sense of duty; but cars, perfumes, chocolates, deodorants, aperients and aperitifs."

The other widespread criticism was that, as professor John Cohen put it, advertisements only tell 'half the truth'. Almost all the contributors said they wanted advertisements to give more information, to be more factual, more honest.

When the series finished, *Campaign* magazine invited J Walter Thompson [JWT; an advertising and communications company] chairman Dr. John Treasure, and me, to respond. In briefest summary, Treasure replied to Mayhew's argument, while I replied to Professor Cohen's. Treasure pointed out that nobody had ever claimed advertising promotes all the good things of life—there are numerous areas of life in which advertising is not involved—but for most people the good things in their lives include food, holidays, clothes, comfort and material possessions—and being able to choose between them. I argued that advertisements could not include all the facts about any product—the very notion is preposterous. So they select those positive facts in which advertisers believe consumers will be interested, and consumers are well aware advertisements are partial, biased in favour of the advertiser.

But their essays revealed how sharply the critics' opinions differed from those of the general population. Just about every market research study on the subject has shown—then as now—that around 80 percent of the British public feel advertising to be a good thing. A survey at that time, *Europe Today*, showed 79 percent of Britons believed advertising to be informative, while 70 percent believed it to be essential. In Britain, during the last half-century surveys about advertising have been remarkably consistent, and remarkably favourable. (This is not true in all countries).

A Blast of Puffery

Intellectuals disagree with the public about many things, but the intellectuals are usually aware of the conflict. The *Campaign* articles made clear the critics felt their views to be so obviously correct that everyone in the country must surely agree with them. This was not so. But understandable.

Hostility to advertising among British intellectuals goes back a long way. In 1843 Thomas Carlyle dubbed it a "deafening blast of puffery," and at the end of that century the Society for Controlling the Abuses of Public Advertising (SCAPA) included among its members such notables as William Morris, Rudyard Kipling, Holman Hunt, Arthur Quiller-Couch and Sir John Millais—as well as Sydney Courtauld and the Fry chocolate family. But even then the public did not follow their leaders. 500 copies of SCAPA's polemical leaflet were printed. Only 30 were sold.

Still, the critics kept up their fire. Many of the attacks were well-worn retreads. But in 1980 Professor Raymond Williams took the arguments a stage further. Williams—an influential Marxist academic, social commentator, critic and novelist—published an essay called "Advertising: The Magic System." Far from being too materialistic, Williams argued, modern adver-

An Assault on Reason

At the most fundamental level, the attacks on advertising are an assault on reason—on man's ability to form concepts and to think in principles—because advertising is a *conceptual* communication to many people at one time about the *conceptual* achievements of others. It is attacked for precisely this aspect of its nature. The goal of advertising is to sell products to consumers, and the means by which this goal is achieved is to communicate what advertisers call the "product concept." An advertisement is itself an abstraction, a concept of what the capitalist has produced. Thus, advertising is a conceptual communication—in a market economy—to self-interested buyers about the self-interested, conceptual achievements of capitalists. To criticize advertising—at the most fundamental level—is to assault man's consciousness.

Jerry Kirkpatrick,
In Defense of Advertising: Arguments from Reason,
Ethical Egoism, and Laissez-Faire Capitalism.
Westport, CT: Quorum Books, 1994.

tising is not materialistic enough, because the images with which advertisements surround goods deliberately detract attention from the goods' material specifications: "If we were sensibly materialist we should find most advertising to be an insane irrelevance," he averred. In the 19th century he said, more or less accurately, advertising was generally factual and informative, except for fraudulent patent medicine and toiletry advertisements, which had already adopted the undesirable practices which later became commonplace. In other words Williams was not attacking all advertising, just most present-day advertisements.

Why, he asked, do advertisements exploit "deep feelings of a personal and social kind?" His answer: because the concentration of economic power into ever larger units forces those units to make human beings consume more and more, in order for the units to stay operative. "The fundamental choice . . . set to us by modern industrial production, is between man as a consumer and man as a user." He argues that usage is continuous—today we might say sustainable—but consumption is inherently destructive. So the emphasis on consumers and consumption, rather than on users and usage, is inherently an emphasis on destruction. This emphasis occurs because destruction is necessary to keep the wheels of industry turning. (How we could use Liquorice Allsorts without consuming them Williams neglects to explain, but we'll let that pass).

Like Christopher Mayhew (and [economist] J.K. [John Kenneth] Galbraith), Williams contended that many laudable human needs—"hospitals, schools, quiet"—are out of phase with an industrialised society. So the industrialised society uses advertising to focus attention on its industrial output, and to detract humanity from its nonindustrial aspirations. This, he says, is why modern advertisements usurp our sexual and emotional desires, attaching them to goods and services. It is akin to the voodoo of the primitive magic man—hence the essay's title: It diverts the tribe toward inessential needs.

A Seductive Argument

At first glance this is a seductive argument. But it is wrong. While the usage of some goods—spectacles, say, or paintings—does not destroy them, the usage of most goods—like Liquorice Allsorts—does destroy them. And this is perhaps fortunate, because "the fundamental choice" is not, as Williams posits, "between man as consumer and man as user", but between man as consumer and man as producer (the male chauvinism is his, not mine). Williams correctly says advertising keeps the industrial wheels turning. But if the industrial wheels stopped turning there would be mass unemployment.

Above all, Williams is wrong because insofar as advertising emphasizes emotional and sexual desires—far less than he supposes—this is not merely because human beings inevitably have emotional relationships with material goods, but because most material goods have no intrinsic value: They are merely means to ends. His emphasis on the specifications of products misses the point: It is functionality which matters. Primitive man did not make spearheads because he needed spearheads: He made spearheads because he needed food and protection. People do not buy drills because they want drills, they buy drills because they want holes. Specifications are only important insofar as they deliver the required benefits. And the benefits may be material, or may be emotional.

Today few critics take issue with advertising as a phenomenon. Instead they focus on individual sectors—alcohol, fattening foods, financial credit or whatever—where the issues are specific, and rather different. Today almost everyone who has examined the issues accepts that advertising does indeed help keep the wheels of industry turning, and hence keeps people in jobs. Today almost everyone accepts that by subsidising the media, advertising helps keep them relatively inexpensive and relatively free from government control. (This, too, is not true in all countries).

The area where contention still rages is how advertising benefits consumers (if at all). But the great French essayist [Michel de] Montaigne hit the spot in his 1595 essay "Of a Defect in Our Policies." How, he asked, can sellers and buyers successfully communicate with each other? And like many other early commentators he believed the principal loser from the lack of communication to be the buyer. Unless buyers know about all the goods on offer, they miss out. And nobody since Montaigne (since ancient Athens come to that) has devised a better way than advertising to bridge this knowledge gap. If consumers did not benefit from advertising, it would not work.

Happily, in Britain we get two-for-the-price-of-one: an economic service—with added creativity (which, again, is not true in all countries). And maybe the creativity is catalysed by the criticisms.

> "Amid the confusion over new media, many advertisers are studying how to make use of word-of-mouth marketing, an age-old form of persuasion."

Advertising Is Too Pervasive

Lucas Conley

Lucas Conley is a contributing writer for Fast Company *and author of* OBD: Obsessive Branding Disorder: The Business of Illusion and the Illusion of Business. *In the following viewpoint, excerpted from* OBD: Obsessive Branding Disorder, *Conley contends that Americans are overwhelmed by the escalating onslaught of advertising and marketing in everyday life. As conventional commercials lose hold, he claims that brands are resorting to aggressive tactics, such as viral marketing, "advertainment" programming, and buying ad space on people's bodies. Conley concludes that such deceptive and invasive marketing ploys erode the public's trust and illustrate the willingness of brands to exploit every opportunity for promotion and profit.*

As you read, consider the following questions:

1. How is buzz marketing misleading, according to Lucas Conley?

2. As stated by Conley, how are brands resorting to cheaper, shorter ads?

3. What is a "sermomercial," as described by Conley?

From advertisements on billboards to newspaper ads, television commercials, online banners, and spam, the average American encounters between three thousand and five thousand ad messages each day, a number that has nearly tripled in the last generation. Sixty-five percent of Americans say they feel "constantly bombarded" by ads; fifty-nine percent see ads as having little relevance to their lives. Yet the ads keep coming.

Increasingly convinced of the importance of image over products and services, brands are devoting greater resources than ever before to their advertising and marketing departments. The hope is that more illusion will generate more interest, but the impact has been the opposite. Instead of learning from more messages, consumers are more often overwhelmed by information. In 2006 U.S. advertisers spent nearly $300 billion—about $10,000 a second—trying to reach us. More alarming than the annual total is the overall trend. Advertisers have spent more in the past decade than they did in the four previous decades *combined*. In 1996 ad spending in the United States was estimated at $175 billion, almost half the amount of today's advertising costs.

Breaking Through the Clutter

With the arrival of blogs, social networking sites, globally interactive video games, and ever-expanding technology, brands are being forced to think beyond the standard thirty-second TV ad to reach their customers. As cheap mass-media advertising, democratized by the Internet and cable TV, makes it possible for even the smallest companies to reach large audiences, more and more ad clutter is generated. Each new attempt to "break through the clutter" only adds more. Extending their reach into the entertainment industry, brands are creating their own shows and video games and opening their own Hollywood studios.

Other brands resort to strong-arming tactics and subversiveness. In return for their ad dollars, some, like Bayer Health-Care, have demanded that magazines print "good news" about their products. Funding for blogs, viral videos, and guerrilla advertising is similarly nebulous, and it's often impossible to distinguish brand propaganda from genuine demonstrations of customer devotion. Amid the confusion over new media, many advertisers are studying how to make use of word-of-mouth marketing, an age-old form of persuasion. Sometimes called buzz marketing, the increasingly formalized field has enlisted millions of brand-sponsored "buzz agents"—everyday folks who, in return for cash or products, will pitch items to anyone willing to listen, often without revealing their motives.

In 1965, a prime-time advertisement aired on NBC, ABC, and CBS would reach 80 percent of women age 18–49 in the United States. Selling was easy: Companies made commercials, networks aired them, and people bought the products. Today network prime-time ratings are 40 percent lower than they were forty years ago. In 1965 a program like *Bonanza*, the western series that topped the weekly ratings, reached 32 million people. It would take two or three of today's most popular network shows to reach the same audience.

"The existing advertising paradigm sucks," lamented Michael Wiley, director of new media for General Motors' Communications Division. "It's woefully inefficient. We spend these huge dollars and we run them on television and we give the consumer very little information."

The problem with commercials isn't only that they offer insufficient information, but that people have little interest in watching them in the first place. By the end of 2007, 25 million of the 100 million families in the United States had shelled out hundreds of dollars for a digital video recorder [DVR], which, like TiVo, enables them to bypass commercials altogether. Another 28 million DVRs were expected to ship worldwide in 2008. Though DVR owners swear by them, the devices are wreaking havoc with TV networks and their advertisers. According to Susan Whiting, the CEO of Nielsen Media Research, their presence eliminated $600 million worth of commercials in 2007 (and at just 1.5 percent of TV advertising, it's safe to say that's a conservative estimate).

TiVo, of course, is not the sole culprit in the decline of television advertising. Today viewers have thousands of channels to choose from, leaving advertisers unsure of where to spend their dollars, while many prime-time shows are available on commercial-free DVDs or are downloadable from iTunes or YouTube.

The Attention Economy

With the arrival of digital technology, media are limited only by our imagination. We have thousands of television channels, billions of Web sites, tens of thousands of songs in our MP3 players, and streaming videos on our phones. But our attention is finite. Any increase in advertising inherently means less time and attention for other parts of our lives. Indeed, an economy based on attention rather than information has been gathering momentum for a decade. "What counts most is what is most scarce now, namely attention," claims Michael Goldhaber in a seminal online article, "The Attention Economy and the Net." The leading authority on the subject, Goldhaber has been writing about the attention economy since 1985. "The attention economy brings with it its own kinds of wealth," he says, "its own class divisions . . . its own forms of property."

As the novelty of each new advertising medium wears off, from ads on parking lot lines to the backs of receipts to paid space on people's foreheads, we accommodate. Naturally, advertisers accommodate too, encroaching deeper into the physical environments we inhabit. And in Goldhaber's attention economy, we can't possibly pay for it all. Even if we're just glancing for half a second (maybe enough time to absorb two or three words) at the thousands of ads we see every day on billboards, the backs of magazines, and in Web banner advertising, we are still spending thirty to sixty minutes every day noticing ads.

Locked in an escalating arms race against advertisers, telemarketers, and data harvesters, 50 million American households signed up for the Do Not Call Registry when it was launched in 2003—10 million of them in the first three days. Today the list includes 145 million phone numbers. The Do Not Call Registry isn't just frustrating to telemarketers; it's also expensive: Fines for companies that break the rules, such as DIRECTV, have reached $5.3 million.

Abandoning telemarketing, salespeople are increasingly approaching us online with a limitless supply of banner ads, pop-ups, and spam. In 2004 Bill Gates famously declared that spam would be "solved" by 2006. Though software intended to block spam is now ubiquitous, plenty of spam manages to filter through to our in-boxes. As much as 90 percent of all e-mail is estimated to be spam—and its overall volume is skyrocketing. According to network security firm Symantec, spam accounted for 78.5 percent of all e-mails in January 2008.

Thanks to initiatives like the Do Not Call Registry and spam blockers, consumers do have an array of defensive options to prevent ad creep. As a result, image-centered brands are forever migrating, buying up advertising space, and promoting brands wherever space is available. Some are reconsidering traditional advertising channels and flooding them with cash and creativity. Saturated by advertising messages, we are bound to allow some to leak through the gaps in our mental filters.

No Space Is Safe

EnVision Marketing Group is proof that no space is safe from the steady creep of sponsored messages, logos, and branding. A Little Rock–based marketing outfit, enVision's promise is clear: to "turn unused space into new profits."

EnVision's target, though not revolutionary, is somewhat novel. First used in the mid-1960s, supermarket conveyor belts have cycled past us in utilitarian obscurity for more than four decades, waiting patiently for an enterprising soul. EnVision's main product, Art-N-Line, is a digitally printed conveyer belt that touts full-color ads. With ten ads per belt, enVision estimates that most customers see each ad two or three times a week. As one enVision promotional slide put it, "Captive audience: exposed to the message frequently." To some, such blatant and unabashed ad creep is just one more example of unchecked consumerism. To date, Kroger, the number one grocery-only chain in the country, has installed the belts in fifty-two Cincinnati locations as well as in stores across Arkansas, Mississippi, and Tennessee.

Though they rarely attract much attention, the advertising industry is brimming with enterprising, insidious gimmicks like enVision's Art-N-Line. EggFusion uses lasers to inscribe ads on eggs. The China-based company 5sai.com squeezes ads into the tiny spaces reserved by people's instant message names. Micro Target Media wraps portable toilets with advertising for Ford and Major League Baseball. Vision Media uses high-pressure water to etch ads into dirty sidewalks and walls. Beach'n Billboard creates drums for imprinting advertisements in sand. Ads are now played on American school buses, while the paper liners used on examination tables in doctors' offices often host advertisements.

Some makers of creeping ads, like Beach'n Billboard, which works in tandem with beach cleaning machines, suggest that they're actually doing a public service as they vie for our attention. Such is the case with Freeload Press, a publishing

company that's opening the doors for obsessive brands to extend their marketing into college textbooks.

"Liberating the textbook" since 2004, Freeload Press has been offering college students free digital textbooks (e-textbooks). The catch is a subtle slew of ads interspersed between algebra formulas and the principles of Accounting 101, pitching brands like FedEx, Pura Vida Coffee, and Culver's, the Midwest restaurant chain famous for its frozen custard and "butterburgers." With increasingly expensive textbooks (the cost has tripled in the last twenty years according to the [U.S.] Government Accountability Office [GAO]), the average student spends about $900 a year on books alone, fueling a $6.5 billion business. More than one hundred U.S. colleges and universities now use Freeload's books. If a few ads can take the pressure off cash-strapped students, it's hard to argue with these colleges and universities for making the books available.

The One-Second Barrier

With so many easy and affordable ways to raise the profile of a company—from spam and online ads triggered by our own Web searches to hundreds of cable channels and falling print advertising rates—well-established brands are struggling to distinguish themselves in the crowd. Ironically, some are actually using shorter, cheaper ads to get attention. Aiming to deliver its message cheaper, faster, and innovatively, General Electric's "One-Second Theater" is an example of one such "blink" (one-, two-, and five-second ads). GE stuffs thirty frames into a single second of TV airtime, crossing its fingers that viewers will record the ads and play them back in slow motion. While these ads are uncommon compared to standard thirty-second spots, both Cadillac and AOL picked up five-second bits.

The story is much the same on the radio, where, instead of "blinks," we hear "adlets." For one-fifth of the cost of a regular radio spot, Clear Channel, owner of 1,200 stations, sells five seconds of airtime. Two seconds cost just 10 percent of the standard rate—between $80 and $160. By stuffing ads into small breaks between songs, marketers hope to grab listeners' attention. (A two-second ad, after all, is almost unavoidable; it's over by the time you reach for the dial.)

The mania of obsessive branding disorder doesn't stop at the one-second barrier either. To raise their brands' profiles, companies have larded brand messages into slivers of a second—or blipverts. Appearing in e-mails, blipverts can flash words—like BUY! BUY!! BUY!!!—in multiple colors, in multiple sizes, and from multiple angles for as briefly as ten milliseconds. According to Richi Jennings, the eagle-eyed blogger who initially spotted the tiny pieces of spam, blipverts are designed to be small enough to slip by image-blocking spam filters unnoticed.

Advertainment

In an effort to make headway in a cluttered landscape, some major brands like Quicksilver, Mountain Dew, Ford, and Budweiser are effectively skipping the traditional advertisement process altogether to create their own films and shows. Known as branded entertainment, or advertainment, in most cases the medium allows brands complete control over how their products are featured. Early in 2007, in a move that aimed to expand its reign from the King of Beers to the king of branded media, Budweiser launched its multichannel network, Bud.TV, boasting exclusive video shorts from A-list stars like Matt Damon and Vince Vaughn, and BudTube, a "channel" that allows users to share homemade video clips, à la YouTube. (The format was essentially a bust: Bud.TV made little news after its launch, and traffic to the site is reported to have dropped off dramatically.)

While still a nascent movement, advertainment has nonetheless attracted a number of unlikely newcomers. OfficeMax created a product-littered sitcom, *Schooled*, for ABC Family; Snickers developed an online show about hip-hop stars turned superheroes; and megapublisher HarperCollins (recently rebranded itself) struck a cozy deal with Fox's *Stacked*, the short-lived television series that featured a baffled Pamela Anderson wandering around a bookstore. (The books and promotional materials lining the walls of the fictional store were all supplied by HarperCollins.) Even Brawny, the paper towel brand, tried its hand at some branded content. Brawny Academy, a competitive online reality show, encouraged women to log on and "watch real husbands like yours learn from the Brawny Man himself."

Though some of the more mainstream examples of branded entertainment have found traction with audiences, consumers haven't warmed to the majority of brands' efforts.

Going Too Far

Every day each of us contributes to the flush of commercial advertising with subtle nods to brands through the clothing we wear, the cars we drive, the coffee we drink. But most of us write off our purchasing decisions as the inevitable by-products of an age of industry: We have to clothe ourselves, and if we're lucky, we can afford to clothe ourselves in brands we like. And so we drape ourselves in a company product, we drive in branded vehicles, we sip grande lattes from the comfort of cushy couches in Starbucks. But our literal, physical bodies have traditionally remained apart from advertising. Clothed in product though they may be, our bodies have retained some sense of sacred space. In the current explosion of advertising, even this taboo seems to have gone by the wayside. Ad space on body parts is regularly auctioned off to the highest bidder. Babies are particularly hot properties. One St. Louis woman auctioned off the rights to sponsor the birth of her child and allowed a tech company to film the birth and post the event online. Her take for wearing company T-shirts and temporarily tattooing her pregnant belly with the company name was $1,000. In 2005 a mother in North Carolina offered to sell ad space on her fifteen-month-old son; she offered a year's worth of advertising for $100,000, with smaller increments of time on offer through her Web site, www.buy jake.com. At the same time, a Connecticut mother named her child GoldenPalace.com in exchange for $15,100 from the eponymous online casino. (GoldenPalace.com also paid $10,000 for a permanent GoldenPalace.com tattoo on a Utah woman's forehead.)

For people willing to put up some advertising at the altar, some companies, 1-800-FLOWERS and Smirnoff among them, have offered wedding sponsorship. With ads on the altar, it was only a matter of time before the sermomercial—the integration of commercial messages into religious sermons—would appear. Chrysler has reached out to African American churchgoers with a gospel tour through fourteen American megachurches. In 2006 Disney gave pastors everywhere the opportunity to win $1,000 and a trip to Europe if they mentioned *The Chronicles of Narnia* from the pulpit.

Clearly our obsession with branding has gone too far when priests are peddling Disney, liquor brands are sponsoring weddings, and mothers are selling the rights to name their children. Such extremes are sobering indications that ad creep and product placement have so polluted our cultural landscape that they've warped fundamental social and cultural institutions.

Above all else, the intent of branding is to sell. If it reshapes society subtly in the process, so much the better for the brand responsible. But the effect of so much branding has been a steady erosion in the public's trust. With each new branding ploy, consumers grow increasingly skeptical. In turn, companies are proving ever more willing to resort to deception and fake advertising to sell products. Such extreme examples of brands bartering in exchange for representation in what were traditionally sacred spaces illustrate an unhealthy willingness to exploit any opportunity if the price is right.

"Our society has sexism so ingrained in it that advertising simply follows suit."

Many Advertisements Are Sexist

Portia

Portia is an industrial and workplace relations lawyer raised in Wellington, New Zealand. In the following viewpoint, Portia charges that the advertising industry regularly depicts scenarios and stereotypes that are sexist and degrading to women in magazines, commercials, and campaigns. She claims that the use of female nudity and overly sexual messages act as a form of propaganda, which objectifies women, condones domestic violence, and reinforces demeaning behaviors and ideas. The author urges critics to challenge sexist advertising by analyzing the ads surrounding them and voicing their complaints to businesses and advertisers.

As you read, consider the following questions:

1. Why is the "Fire Ho's" dance party promotion offensive, in Portia's view?

2. According to the author, what is "porno chic"?

Portia, "Sexist Advertising," *Muse Feminist Magazine*, October 2005. All content copyright © 2005 Muse Feminist Magazine. Reproduced by permission.

3. What is the goal of sexist advertising, as stated by the author?

Sexist advertising—the definitive example that society is still laden with masculine values and that people accept sexist advertising as a legitimate form of commercial communication. Sexist advertising comes in all shapes and forms, such as reinforcing gender stereotypes and gender roles, using gratuitous female nudity or sex to sell unrelated products, and by marginalising women from advertising and its industry.

Sexist advertising and the sexualisation of women's bodies emanates from both problems with the advertising industry and society. These problems stem from a wee institution called patriarchy. Our society has sexism so ingrained in it that advertising simply follows suit. Therefore, images that objectify and degrade women's bodies are accepted as legitimate for advertising, under the guise of portraying a particular product (and therefore the consumer) as simply sexy, seductive and attractive to the opposite sex.

Serious Social Impacts

There are serious social impacts from this kind of advertising back on society—unrealistic expectations of women's bodies and resulting body image problems, sexual and domestic violence, and sexism being reinforced as an acceptable form of behaviour. Many forms of media such as magazines and television stations financially benefit from these sexist advertisements, as they gain the majority of their revenue from the companies who place ads with them. A major concern with sexist advertising is the simple fact that it becomes so normalised that we don't even notice it (either because it's subconscious, dressed up as artistic or because it's so widespread).

Now I'm a fan of calling a spade a spade, so I'm going to go out on a limb here and say that sexist advertising is simply a form of propaganda. Let's look at this from an academic point of view—in [the book] *Propaganda and Persuasion*, propaganda is defined as disseminating or promoting particular ideals, with the objective of endeavouring to reinforce or modify the attitudes or behaviour of a particular audience. In fact, they argue that advertising campaigns are by definition "systematic propaganda", and label it "ubiquitous". In any case, it can certainly be said that advertising is a form of communication, and a form of dissemination of ideas (whether commercial or political ideas). Advertising aims to convince consumers of the worth of the company and its services or products, with the goal of persuading the consumer to buy the services and products of that company. Essentially, to reinforce the "brand" and modify the behaviour of the consumer to choose that particular brand.

The images that get used in advertising are therefore chosen for a reason, because they either symbolise a particular message or idea the advertiser wishes to promote, or because they reflect the consumer in some way—their image, their attitude, their style. Advertising seeks to draw consumers in a number of ways, but generally makes the product desirable by using images that trigger something in the consumer's mind so that they remember it favourably. As [authors Garth] Jowett and [Victoria] O'Donnell explain, it is "a series of appeals, symbols and statements deliberately designed to influence the receiver of the message toward the point of view desired by the communicator and to act in some specific way as a result of receiving the message. . . ."

Here in lies the rub—we are being subconsciously enticed to buy products by companies who believe that it is okay to use women's bodies in a sexual way to make their brand cool, hip and sexy. And not only are men buying into these products because they are identifying with the product or brand, because the sexist 'propaganda' echoes their own perceptions about women, women's roles, and the proper image a woman should have, but women are too. Often women don't realise their sexual appeal is being exploited by the company to their detriment in society and to the company's financial benefit.

You may be wondering how this fits in with the 'Wellington/New Zealand' context. Sexist advertising and the sexualisation of women's bodies in advertisements is extremely common now. The images accompanying this article are some examples that the *Muse* [magazine] team photographed on billboards simply walking around Wellington one afternoon. The images mostly promote dance parties or music events, and the one I found most offensive was the "Fire Ho's" which used the play on words 'ho' (short for "whore") and "hose," i.e. fire hose. The image depicts a woman dressed in a skimpy firefighter's outfit holding a hose with legs suggestively spread. And what does this have to do with the gig we asked? We should have read the byline—"the girls are turnin' up the heat"—it all makes sense now (???!!). Another was for a medical-themed dance party, or that's the impression we got from the poster, which featured a porn-star nurse sitting on the amp. These advertisements are a pretty weak excuse to use a picture of a sexed-up woman

On a further inquiry, I looked into some magazines, and out of one issue of *Marie Claire* alone, I found fourteen advertisements that used women's bodies in a sexual way (either unrelated to the product or barely related by dint of it being 'skin care'). The ads in *Marie Claire* that I particularly found offensive were two Elle MacPherson lingerie ads which were part of a campaign featuring photos taken from angles imitating a peeping tom, voyeur or stalker. These images never showed the female model's face (but always the male model's), and involved dynamics of power imbalance. This included the female model being placed in a vulnerable or sexual position.

Porno Chic

The use of women's sexuality and the use of gratuitous female nudity in advertisements [has] been labelled "porno chic" by a

Internalizing Stereotypes

Advertising images do not cause these problems, but they contribute to them by creating a climate in which the marketing of women's bodies—the sexual sell and dismemberment, distorted body image ideals and the use of children as sex objects—is seen as acceptable.

There is the real tragedy that many women internalize these stereotypes and learn their "limitations," thus establishing a self-fulfilling prophecy. If one accepts these mythical and degrading images, to some extent one actualizes them. By remaining unaware of the profound seriousness of the ubiquitous influence, the redundant message and the subliminal impact of advertisements, we ignore one of the most powerful "educational" forces in the culture—one that greatly affects our self-images, our ability to relate to each other, and effectively destroys any awareness and action that might help to change that climate.

Jean Kilbourne,
"Beauty . . . and the Beast of Advertising,"
Media & Values, Winter 1990.

Paris media watchdog group, and even within the advertising industry in France it is accepted that "nudity is invariably an excuse for bankruptcy of ideas". However, porno chic has been seen to represent economic optimism and liberation from confining societal (advertising) stereotypes. Advertisers argue they should be allowed to shock their audience, make their campaigns a bit raunchier and show that ultimately their brand is edgy and at the front of fashion and culture. They probably don't even think about the consequences of using naked or semi-naked female bodies in sexual or suggestive positions to advertise shoes (just look at the Overland shoes ads on their Web site), or jeans (Levi's is pretty bad at doing this), or perfume, cosmetics or skin-care products like tanning oil and soap. You can be certain advertising executives don't wake up in the morning and say, "I wonder how my advertising campaign for Brand X beer impacts women's body image or men's view of women?" But when they pick images of women that are sexual they do so because it is what has always been done, because our patriarchal society dictates that the advertising industry employs male values of beauty and attractiveness and male ways of communicating or portraying people.

Each day we are faced with advertisements of a sexual nature, regardless of the product. The goal of this kind of propaganda, this commercial communication, is that if we buy this product we can look like the model, we will experience fulfilment by partaking in that brand's experience, we will be sexy and seductive like the woman in the ad. Why should we swallow that crap? We need to realise that this advertising is plain old sexist, and that in New Zealand there are rules about these kinds of images. The Advertising Standards Authority [ASA] has a set of codes for all forms of advertising and all subject matters. Of particular importance is its code for advertising using people—specifically, "Advertisements should not employ sexual appeal in a manner which is exploitative and degrading of any individual or group of people in society to promote the sale of products or services. In particular people should not be portrayed in a manner which uses sexual appeal simply to draw attention to an unrelated product".

If you see advertising that you think is offensive because it uses a nude or seminude woman in a sexual way, then make a complaint. The company can be forced to remove the advertisement if your complaint is upheld, and one complaint can be enough to do this—you don't need ten people to complain about the same thing (although this probably helps!). Take action, challenge sexist advertising. Take notice of your surroundings and analyse the advertisements—the only way to change the attitudes of advertising companies is if we tell them that sexist advertising is not okay, and that we are tired of the objectification of our bodies in order for companies . . . [to] make a profit.

> "The admen behind much of the adver-
> tising feminists labelled as sexist and
> damaging were often women."

Many Allegedly Sexist Advertisements Were Created by Women

Joy Parks

Joy Parks has been an advertising copywriter for two decades. In the following viewpoint, she proposes that women have been be- hind purportedly sexist advertising. Parks contends that through- out the history of American advertising, women have acted as copywriters, art directors, and home economists, hired to create effective advertisements and marketing for women. In fact, some of the key players in the New York advertising world during the mid-twentieth century were female, she adds, and can be cred- ited with campaigns and slogans that now seem dated and con- descending. Parks states that fewer women are at the creative helm in advertising today, and sexism in the industry must be challenged.

Joy Parks, "Mad Men, Mad Women," *Herizons*, vol. 22, Spring 2009, pp. 22, 25–27.

As you read, consider the following questions:

1. According to Joy Parks, what are Helen Lansdowne Resor's achievements in advertising?

2. As stated by Parks, what percentage of consumer spending do experts believe is influenced by women?

3. What positive signs are consumers showing against sexist advertising, in Parks's view?

Discussions about women and advertising have been reignited thanks to the level of unapologetic sexism portrayed in the award-winning drama *Mad Men*, a television series about a 1960s advertising agency. But who really was responsible for creating those damaging gender stereotypes in advertising?

It's easy to blame it on the mad men. The first season of the hit AMC TV series received 16 Emmy nominations and was the first basic cable show to win the coveted award for best drama—plus, it won five others. A period piece depicting the dark side of the lives of senior executives in a New York advertising agency in 1960, *Mad Men* has inspired a retro trend in designer menswear and a fascination with Lucky Strikes and cocktails. It has also unleashed much discussion and debate—online and off—about the show's depiction of the unmitigated sexism in the 1960s workplace. As TV critic and blogger Aaron Barnhart characterized it, it speaks to a time when "men were men and women were their secretaries."

While there are plenty of complex female characters on the show, the men dominate with their infidelity, overt double standards and unchecked sexual harassment. In addition, the creative team at the fictional Sterling Cooper agency spend much time debating "what women want" and how to sell it [to] them, unleashing a level of misogyny that has pulled scabs off old wounds regarding how women have been portrayed in mainstream advertising.

Feminism—for all of these reasons, and then some—has had a long-standing feud with the advertising industry. While gallons of ink [have] been spilled on the subject of gender stereotypes in advertising, it was Betty Friedan who fired the first shot, placing much of the blame for women's unhappiness on America's post-war consumer society, and especially on advertisers' exploitation of women.

"It is their millions which blanket the land with persuasive images, flattering the American housewife, diverting her guilt and disguising her growing emptiness. They have done this so successfully, employing the techniques and concepts of modern social science, and transposing them into those deceptively simple, clever, outrageous ads and commercials, that an observer of the American scene today accepts as fact that the great majority of American women have no ambition other than to be housewives. If they are not responsible for sending women home, they are surely responsible for keeping them there."

But Were All the Admen Really Men?

No, says Juliann Sivulka! In her brand new book *Ad Women: How They Impact What We Need, Want and Buy*, she reveals that the admen behind much of the advertising feminists labelled as sexist and damaging were often women.

Sivulka takes an in-depth and quite fascinating look at the history of American advertising, from the late 19th century to just a few years ago, linking evolutions in the industry to major societal upheavals in 1880, the 1920s and the 1970s. She uncovers how and why the advertising and marketing communications industry went from a handful of women employees to one in which women far outnumber men.

The trend toward female employees was in direct relation to a new understanding of the marketplace. As women began to be viewed as consumers, originally the keepers of the household money and later of their own income, ad agencies and their clients recognized the value of employing women who would, it was believed, better know what would motivate a woman to buy something and, with this insider knowledge, be able to create effective advertising.

In the early 20th century, countless women received a pay-cheque and a certain amount of career fulfillment through their work in ad agencies—as writers, mainly, but also as media buyers, art directors and home economists who advised manufacturers on new household devices.

One of the most influential of these women was Helen Lansdowne Resor, the daughter of a divorced single mother and the very first copywriter hired at J Walter Thompson [JWT], an agency still regarded as an international expert in gender-related marketing. Resor developed an emotional hard-sell technique that spoke to the consumer's needs rather than the product's features—a revolutionary approach at that time. She wrote in a friendly, advice-driven style and made use of psychology, copy-testing and sampling—elements new to an industry still in its infancy.

Resor also built the women's editorial department to teach other women employees how to create effective advertising for women. Through this group, the J Walter Thompson agency developed the careers of more women than any other early agency. It hired women for the very quality they were expected to subjugate in order to succeed in most other fields—their outsider perspective as women.

The women who were part of the women's editorial department viewed their work as a feminist activity. Outside of work, they belonged to suffragette leagues, the National Women's Party [NWP]—an early feminist organization founded in 1917 that fought for the passage of a constitutional amendment ensuring women's suffrage—and the League of Women Voters; they published articles, ran magazines and spoke on feminist issues or other related causes. While doing so, they may have led lives that were very different than the housewives they were selling to. They sincerely believed they were helping to make women's lives easier, a belief shared by the women who joined other agencies modelled on J Walter Thompson's success and who participated in creating the advertising that later feminists would criticize so vehemently....

Did They or Didn't They?

Despite what *Mad Men* would have you believe, in the late 1950s and early 1960s several of the most powerful people in the New York advertising world were women—three of the better known being Mary Wells Lawrence, Shirley Polykoff and Jane Trahey. Wells's agency, Wells Rich Greene, was responsible, in 1971, for the justifiably loathed "I'm Cheryl, Fly Me" ads for the now defunct National Airlines, a campaign often touted as a classic example of sexism in advertising. Polykoff, working for Foote, Cone & Belding, created the long-running "Does She or Doesn't She" hair colour ads for Clairol. While they now seem dated, condescending and ageist, originally they were meant to encourage women's self-expression.

Of the three, only Trahey demonstrated any feminist sensibility. The owner of Trahey & Co., she rose from a small Chicago in-house agency to eventually become chief of copy at Nieman Marcus in Dallas, then returned to New York to open her own shop. In addition to award-winning ad copy, several books and plays, including the 1962 novel *The Trouble with Angels*, which became a major motion picture, she also penned *Jane Trahey on Women and Power* in 1978. While it, too, seems dated now—since competing with men is considered passé by current feminist standards—this was practical feminism, a how-to book that used humour and insider grit to help women navigate the sexism of the business world. As she wrote in the introduction: "I don't think there's any point in hashing over the sociological, economic, psychological reasons why women don't have any more power in the world than

Silly Men

Silly men. You can't take them anywhere.

If they're not messing up your house, running into glass doors or trying in vain to outsmart an air freshener, you'll find them eating the inedible or falling down for no reason whatsoever.

At least, that's what some advertisers would have you believe. More and more marketers are trying to tap into the overwhelming buying power of wives and mothers at the expense of their other halves. Dads are dumb, boyfriends are bumbling and husbands are utterly hopeless as brands strive to relate to women by showing men as especially goofy or incompetent.

Susan Krashinsky,
"Why Men in Ads Are Dumb, Goofy or Completely Inept,"
Globe and Mail, *August 7, 2009.*

they do. We've been told a hundred times what's keeping us down. What we need are ways to change the situation."

The New Women's Market

While it may be hard to believe, there remain legions of re- searchers today concerned with the still-elusive women's mar- ket. According to Andrea Gardner, author of *The 30-Second Seduction: [How Advertisers Lure Women Through Flattery, Flirtation, and Manipulation]*, the mother market alone has five behavioural groups and marketing experts Carol Osborne and Mary Brown claim there are three different kinds of women baby boomers. Women are still viewed as the primary consumer, and women baby boomers in particular are unique because they are the first generation to have their own in- comes in significant numbers. Like previous generations of women, they control household spending, but also have significant personal money. According to experts, women directly or indirectly initiate or influence 80 percent of all consumer spending.

In business, money talks. Advertisers want a financial return on their investment, which means the sheer number of baby boomer women and their significant consumer clout should have the power to force changes in how marketing portrays them. But that isn't happening.

Fewer Women Today

With all this information on who women are, what they want and what they have to spend, one would expect advertising directed at them to be less sexist, more diverse and less youth-oriented. But the majority of it isn't. That's because—unlike the earlier part of the past century, when agencies recognized the usefulness of having women craft sales messages for women—most of the decision makers and creative people in agencies today are men in their 20s and early 30s. In fact, it's getting harder to find women in upper creative positions.

The U.S. Equal Employment Opportunity Commission [EEOC] in 2003 noted that women far outnumber men in agencies, at 65.8 percent of jobs. But their status recedes with rank. Women hold 76.7 of clerical positions, 58.2 percent of all professional positions and 47 percent of upper management positions. But on the creative side, where messaging decisions get made, they don't even come close to the early 1920s numbers, or even those of the 1960s *Mad Men* era. Of *Adweek's* 33 top agencies, only four have women as their senior creative director.

In November 2007, the *Globe and Mail*, in an interview with Lorraine Tao and Elspeth Lynn, founding partners of the ad agency Zig, referred to their firm as having a "fun, pop-feminist sensibility." The women had been creative partners at other agencies and their own small Canadian shop was boasting clients like Molson, IKEA, Best Buy, Virgin Mobile and Unilever.

Notably, the duo produced a commercial for Kellogg's Special K cereal that depicted average men deriding aspects of their bodies using classic female scripts. It delivered a strong message about advertising and women's insecurities about body image.

Buying into a Better Future

There have been a few ad campaigns in recent years to get it right. Dove's "Real Beauty" campaign, shot by legendary photographer Annie Leibovitz, featured real women with real rolls, cellulite and wrinkles. The "Real Beauty" campaign, created by Ogilvy & Mather, also included the YouTube ad Evolution, which used time-lapse photography to demonstrate how ordinary women are made to look perfectly fake for ads. The campaign also saw the company set up a Self-Esteem Fund to support programs designed to encourage young girls to develop a healthy body image.

In 2006, the company commissioned a report in nine countries, including Canada, asking nearly 1,500 mature women what was wrong with the advertising directed to them. According to Sharon MacLeod, brand building director for Dove, "75 percent of women over 50 report that antiaging ads often portray unrealistic images of women over 50. Women are regularly confronted with messages that they should minimize, reduce, eliminate or defy the natural signs of aging."

Ironically, the body-image-positive Dove ads were at the centre of a boycott by the American Family Association [AFA] for their over-sexualization of women. Leave it to the radical right to turn women's words against them.

Still, Unilever received far more kudos than criticism for Dove's marketing. But will the trend continue? According to media and gender issues expert Jean Kilbourne, author of

Can't Buy My Love: How Advertising Changes the Way We Think and Feel and producer of the award-winning documentary *Killing Us Softly*, "It all depends on how much soap the ads sell."

What If Women Mattered?

What will it take to change how advertisers often portray women? One positive sign is that consumers are complaining. According to the Advertising Standards Council's 2007 annual report, depicting women in a derogatory manner was one of four prime issues cited in the 1,445 complaints the council received, a 40 percent increase compared to 2006. The self-regulating council found that 5.7 percent of the ads cited in 2007 complaints contravened the Canadian Code of Advertising Standards. Those advertisers were asked to amend or withdraw their advertisements.

Women must continue to demand more realistic, more intelligent messages, or simply refuse to buy products by advertisers who create messages that offend them. As Andrea Gardner, author of *The 30-Second Seduction*, writes: "In the end, the ones who have the power to create that shift are today's powerful female consumers, the ones who buy from companies that treasure them."

> *"Agencies, publications, channels and digital content providers are building brand partnerships and developing initiatives to improve people's lives and the health of our planet."*

Cause Marketing Is Beneficial

Richard Westlund

Cause marketing *is a term to describe the partnership between a for-profit and a nonprofit organization and other commercial involvement in charity or social issues. In the following viewpoint, Richard Westlund states that effective cause marketing can benefit society, consumers, and commerce. He suggests that cause marketing can strengthen a brand's emotional appeal to consumers and initiate socially responsible expansion. It can also improve corporate reputations, Westlund says. But he advises that companies choose a cause that is relevant and aligned with its long-term objectives, or cause marketing can backfire. Westlund is a writer for AdweekMedia.*

As you read, consider the following questions:

1. What examples of missteps in cause marketing does Richard Westlund provide?

2. What measures did *TIME* magazine and David Refkin take in their efforts for sustainable forestry, as described by Westlund?

3. What did a survey indicate about consumers' responses to cause marketing ads, according to the viewpoint?

Time Inc. supports sustainable forestry practices. *SELF* magazine this spring [2008] is highlighting individual examples of "Women Doing Good." NBC Universal is encouraging viewers to "go green." It seems like everyone in the media world today is involved with a worthy cause. Agencies, publications, channels and digital content providers are building brand partnerships and developing initiatives to improve people's lives and the health of our planet.

But why is one cause marketing program a success, while others are ignored, or even worse?

Crafting an effective cause marketing initiative is like finding the right path through a swamp. Step too far toward the cause, and your shareholders may complain. Focus too much on the business, and watchdog activists will start screaming. And as any marketer that's been accused of "greenwashing" will tell you, the result of a "bad" cause marketing campaign can become a big ugly "carbon footprint" in the press.

So before you jump on the bandwagon, some soul-searching is required. "Ask yourself why you're doing this," says Valerie Davis, CEO [chief executive officer] and principal of EnviroMedia, an Austin, Texas, firm. "Think about what you want to get out of this. Think about the business goals first, and then educate your employees, from the boardroom to the showroom. Get your own house in order before you're ready to go out and shoot a TV spot."

Because cause marketing requires a significant commitment of resources—time, talent and funds—a good starting point is to ask a simple question: What's the return on investment?

For some media companies and brands, the focus might be strengthening that all-important emotional connection to consumers or to a B2B [business to business] audience. Other players are seeking a positive way to grow a franchise, expand a product portfolio and generate additional revenue. And, yes, there are also companies with altruistic motives, where making an impact is the core mission.

"You need to find the right balance," says Sara Snow, a green lifestyle expert and host of *Get Fresh with Sara Snow* on Discovery Network. "You can't focus solely on business and personal gain without giving back and helping causes not related to your pocketbook."

Fascinating Case Studies

How those intersecting motives play out in the corporate social responsibility (CSR) arena makes for some fascinating case studies. For example, Harry Woods, partner with Woods Witt Dealy & Sons in New York, helped Sundance Channel develop "The Green," a three-hour prime-time programming block now in its second season.

"We think green awareness has advanced from the 'scary smokestack' stage, through the '100 easy tips you can use' stage, and into the attractive lifestyle space," he says. "Green has become a more interesting way of life for an increasing number of people—as well as brands and marketers."

On a larger scale, Discovery Communications is rebranding its Discovery Home Channel as Planet Green on June 4 [2008]. "For us, it's all about motivating people to take an active role in a new conversation about the future of our planet," says Eileen O'Neill, president and general manager. "It made sense for us to make the change at this time in the social landscape."

With more than 250 hours of original green lifestyle programming, Planet Green will [include] celebrities such as Tom Bergeron, Emeril Lagasse, Tom Brokaw and Tom Green. Discovery has also beefed up its online content with the launch of planetgreen.com and the recent acquisition of treehugger .com.

"We expect the network will provide a high entertainment value, activating people who are already interested in the green space," says O'Neill. "As viewers get excited, we offer them online platforms that are ideal for conversations, connectivity, localization and commerce."

On the print side, National Geographic expanded its franchise this spring [2008] with the launch of *Green Guide*, its first service magazine. "We strive to inspire people to care about the planet," says Stephen P. Giannetti, senior VP [vice president] and group publisher. "That differentiates us from other media companies."

To launch its new publication, National Geographic took an organic approach, first telling national POS [point-of-sale] retailers like Whole Foods about its new product. Throw-ins and bind-ins were incorporated in the company's other magazines, promoting the *Green Guide* to subscribers.

To intrigue the media, advertisers and green-savvy VIPs [very important persons] like Al Gore and Robert Redford, National Geographic's marketing department sent a package of organic foods and wine in a reusable shopping bag. It included an "un-event" invitation made with garden seed-embedded paper so recipients could actually start growing their own gardens.

With the second issue due in June [2008], the *Green Guide* is already meeting its revenue goals, thanks to a host of advertisers from automotive to natural food companies. "The world is coming to National Geographic wanting to talk about their corporate and social responsibilities around the environment," says Giannetti. "The *Green Guide* has allowed companies with smaller budgets to get this message out."

Giannetti looks at the *Green Guide*'s online component as an important extension to the company's Webby Award–winning Web site www.nationalgeographic.com. "What's becoming important in the green space is the ability to social network online and talk," he says. "Companies of all sizes want to know 'How can I get people to talk about my brand and what I'm doing for the environment?' We want people to come to our site, network and share ideas."

Reputation Matters

Another motivating force for brands and media companies is the not-so-small matter of corporate reputation—an intangible asset that makes up more than 50 percent of a company's true market cap, according to Anthony Johndrow, managing director of the Reputation Institute in New York.

"Most companies are feeling the impetus to do something good," he says. "A few years ago, you couldn't have started a conversation about corporate reputation in the U.S., where we have [focused on] one bottom line."

To become a better corporate citizen and an effective cause marketer, whatever you do needs to be relevant to your business and your long-term vision. That means you can't just go out and pick any old cause.

A retail bank, for instance, should focus on greenbacks, not greenery. "Banks help people finance homes and educations and start new businesses—that's their space," says Johndrow. "Hearing banks talk about how green they're going just doesn't make sense in terms of messaging." On the other hand, an energy company today should be talking about alternative fuels and its vision of the future.

In the media industry, Johndrow says, it's not always clear which cause will have the most beneficial impact on reputation—although the task may be easier for tightly focused publications, channels and brands than it is for media conglomerates.

"As a result, the reputation landscape is tainted with screwups," Johndrow says. "Think about a big powerful media

Give from the Heart

Cause marketing works best when you and your employees feel great about the help you're providing to a nonprofit group. So work with an organization you and your team believe in, whether that means supporting the fight on behalf of a national health issue or rescuing homeless pets. What matters most to you, your team and your customers? You'll work hard to make a difference when you give from the heart.

Kim T. Gordon, "Cause Marketing Matters to Consumers," Entrepreneur.com, October 14, 2008. www.entrepreneur.com.

company prosecuting students for downloading songs or fighting with writers. Meanwhile, the consumer is saying, 'Why should I want them to make money?' It's not the best way to improve your reputation."

Natural Alignment

But there are many examples of natural alignment. Some voracious users of paper products, such as publishing companies, have gotten behind the forestry management cause. "We've been active in the sustainable forestry program for almost 10 years, looking at the whole supply chain," says David Refkin, director of sustainable development for Time Inc. The company's use of certified sustainable wood products has risen from 25 percent in 2002 to 70 percent last year.

Time Inc. also launched a study on the biodiversity of Canadian forests with supplier UPM, the University of Moncton and other partners to assess the impact of harvesting trees on songbird populations, with a full report expected in 2011.

Time is participating in a working group with other large paper users, including HP [Hewlett-Packard], Staples, Nike,

Bank of America, McDonald's and Wal-Mart. "You learn by talking to other people, seeing their challenges and coming up with innovative solutions," he says.

Refkin even goes to logging camps to talk to the big guys—lumberjacks—as well as the big companies. "At one meeting in Michigan's Upper Peninsula, there were 375 loggers who wanted to eat me for breakfast," he recalls. "But you have to engage in a two-way dialogue, and it's better to hear from people directly than through intermediaries."

Most media companies are far less concerned about the source of their paper—and that could be a big mistake, says Dave Deger, VP [vice president] of marketing for Ohio-based NewPage Corp., the largest coated paper manufacturer in North America.

"Nobody wants to find themselves at a press conference explaining why the company's catalogs or year-end reports were printed on paper tied to potentially illegal logging practices, unfair labor or polluting mills," says Deger. "Reputations can be ruined in just a few minutes."

NewPage is launching a new campaign, "Paper Tells a Story," to educate paper buyers and specifiers about verifying sources of origin and sustainability protocols, such as the Sustainable Forestry Initiative® standard. "Historically, corporate marketers, agencies and printers didn't always have to think about the product their marketing messages are printed on from a sustainability perspective," he says. "We feel it's important to get on the radar of the advertising and design community, as well as companies that sell paper."

The initiative uses direct mail and advertising to drive people to a new microsite. Deger calls it an on-ramp for creative types to learn about paper sourcing and production via a blog element, viral videos and podcasts. "As a paper company ourselves, we see direct mail married to online content as an optimum approach," he adds.

Consumers React

Two years ago, *SELF* magazine partnered with Latitude Research to learn what consumers really think about cause marketing. "We wanted to learn more ourselves, while knowing that our marketing partners could also use this information," says Kimberly Kelleher, VP and publisher. Key findings of the survey, which canvassed 1,700 women:

- 70 percent said purchasing products from "good" brands makes them feel they're socially responsible. "It's providing her with a huge emotional benefit," says Cynthia Walsh, executive director of marketing, who developed the survey.

- 71 percent felt "good" purchases let them support a cause without much effort, taking it off a to-do list. "Women have always been multitaskers," Walsh says. "Now they want to see their dollars multitasked as well."

- Respondents were willing to pay 6.1 percent more for a brand affiliated with a "good" message. "Companies measure how much people pay for loyalty and awareness," Walsh says. "This can be layered on top of those findings—putting a 'good' message on top of the loyalty value—and a brand could be worth 10 percent more in the consumer's eye."

- Positive response rates to "good" ads were far higher than to traditional ads. "Cause marketing ads really did change consumers' perceptions of companies," says Walsh. While you don't want to walk away from the functional benefits of traditional advertising, this approach adds a new level of emotional connection—a humanizing effect."

- 32 percent expect companies to do good things now; however, 85 percent hope that companies will eventually get more involved in good causes. "We see that gap closing rather quickly," says Kelleher. "Right now, it seems like we're at a tipping point for companies to make a statement in this space."

Since releasing the survey last fall [2007], *SELF* has been putting its research into action. In April [2008], the magazine asked readers to nominate "Women Doing Good," a program that rewards four winners with $10,000 each for their initiatives.

Start Small

As any marketer knows, the biggest challenges to any CSR [corporate social responsibility] initiative are consumer inertia, skepticism and simple lack of time. As Snow says, "Everyone is overextended, trying to do too many things at once. So you have to make a commitment and build it into your priorities."

Then come the basics: setting objectives, building consensus among employees, shareholders and other stakeholders, preparing the message and measuring results.

It's a tall order—but it doesn't have to be all-consuming. "Start small, and ramp up," says Kelleher. "Let things build over time. And if you make mistakes, at least they'll be smaller ones."

After all, the big issues aren't going to go away any time soon. "We see continued momentum throughout the green space," says O'Neill. "And we all need to invest ourselves in long-term solutions."

*"Vagaries [surround] ever-ubiquitous
cause-related marketing."*

Cause Marketing Is
Not Beneficial

Anne Kingston

*Cause marketing is a business partnership, initiative, or strategy
that is associated with a charitable or social issue. In the following viewpoint, Anne Kingston purports that cause marketing
may be problematic and unbeneficial. She highlights the main
concerns of detractors: Cause marketing encourages people to engage in charity, altruism, or activism solely through consumer
choices and can create apathy toward enduring global problems.
The author speculates that fund-raising may not be the primary
objective of a cause marketing campaign. Kingston is a senior
writer for* Maclean's, *a Canadian weekly current affairs magazine.*

As you read, consider the following questions:

1. According to Anne Kingston, what accusation has been
   leveled against the Red campaign?

2. In Samantha King's opinion, why is cause marketing
   "safe" for consumers?

Anne Kingston, "The Trouble with Buying for a Cause," *Maclean's*, March 26, 2007. Reproduced by permission.

3. What statement did buylesscrap.org make about cause marketing?

When Bono unveiled the global brand Red at the World Economic Forum at Davos in January 2006, it was heralded as a bold new model in cause-related marketing, a win-win-win scenario destined for case study in the *Harvard Business Review*: Launch partners the Gap, Apple, Motorola, Giorgio Armani, Converse and American Express would donate a percentage of profits to the Geneva-based Global Fund to Fight AIDS, Tuberculosis and Malaria; shoppers could snap up stylish Red iPod nanos, Red MOTORAZR V3 phones, Red mud-cloth Converse sneakers and Red Gap Empowe(RED) T-shirts, buoyed by the knowledge they were fighting AIDS in Africa; the Global Fund would receive publicity and funds from a new donor base without spending a penny. Bono framed Red as a "commercial imperative" that would create a "sustainable" income stream for the fund. "Philanthropy is like hippie music, holding hands," the U2 front man said. "Red is more like punk rock, hip hop; this should feel like hard commerce."

A soft launch in March [2006] was followed by a splashy, celebrity-riddled rollout in October [2006]. Oprah championed Red, Chris Rock proclaimed "Use Red, nobody's dead" for Motorola, Steven Spielberg donned a Red Gap leather jacket, his first-ever commercial endorsement. Now, a mere five months later, Red is mired in censure amid speculation that its partner companies are bleeding its signature colour, while doing comparatively little for charity. "Bono & Co. spend up to $100 mil on marketing" blazed a headline in last week's [in March 2007] *Advertising Age* [*Ad Age*, for short] above a story that claimed the companies associated with Red had forked out a fortune to market the brand while the Global Fund received just US$18 million. This week, the magazine ran a rebuttal by Bobby Shriver, Red's CEO [chief executive officer] and driving force, claiming the brand had netted

US$25 million on total profits in excess of US$60 million, five times the amount the Global Fund had received from the private sector since its inception in 2001. He said the US$100 million marketing figure is "wrong, by more than 50 percent," and noted Red generated traffic for its vendors as well as awareness of AIDS in Africa. In an editor's note, *Advertising Age* said it stood by its story.

Shopping for a Better World

The dustup highlights the vagaries surrounding ever-ubiquitous cause-related marketing. Shopping for a better world is built in to the consumer ethic: Buying a pink KitchenAid mixer promises a cure for breast cancer; a bottle of Starbucks's Ethos water will deliver clean water to "children of the world," Ben & Jerry's new flavor "Stephen Colbert Americone Dream" donates more vaguely to "various charities." Samantha King, a Queen's University professor and author of *Pink Ribbons, Inc.: Breast Cancer and the Politics of Philanthropy*, a critical look at the commercialization of breast cancer, says that within the nonprofit sector a marketing outlay of $3 for every $1 brought in is the norm. Raising money isn't always the primary objective of cause marketing, says Jocelyne Daw, vice president of marketing and social engagement at Imagine Canada and author of *Cause Marketing for Nonprofits*. "It can be an effective way to partner with a company, piggyback on their marketing and benefit from their brand and their reach to a range of consumers," she says. King's concern is that those consumers can fall prey to an I-gave-at-the-Gap passivity that reduces charity to the cause du jour [of the day]. Whatever happened to the rain forest? As a cause, it has been upstaged by AIDS in Africa which, too, is destined to meet with consumer ennui [boredom]. King also notes corporations' need to sell product dictates that the messages surrounding the cause tend to be pretty safe: "They want to comfort rather than get people thinking."

Such skepticism underlies the Red backlash. It can be traced to the Web site buylesscrap.org, which floated the US$100-million Red marketing figure and sparked the *Ad Age* story. Set up by a group of San Francisco designers and artists, the site condemns "the ti(red) notion that shopping is a reasonable response to human suffering," and offers direct links to charities, including the Global Fund. Cofounder Ben Davis, who faults Red for lack of transparency, admits the US$100-million marketing figure was a guesstimate. Davis has coined the term "causumer" to describe the shopper navigating another level of confusion in the consumer decision-making process. Being a "causumer" can be a positive market force, he says, provided information exists. "It's not enough to say 'Save lives, buy this shirt.' It's not enough to say '50 percent of gross profits go to the cause,' because that's not a real number to anyone. That could be nothing." Red vendors, who have five-year contracts, donate some 40 percent of undefined "profits" directly to the Global Fund. Individual company donations are not released. What each product generates for the fund varies: Apple donates $10 from the sale of every Red iPod nano, for example, and Gap offers "50 percent of profits" from Red merchandise.

Building a Brand

Speaking from his Los Angeles office, Shriver says Red isn't targeted at "causumers." "Shoppers don't perceive buying a T-shirt as a charitable act," he says. "They're buying a cool T-shirt." He presents the Red brand as infiltrating the commercial transaction. Money donated is essentially found, just as marketing money was earmarked. "The idea was, 'you're going to buy a cell phone anyway, so why not buy a Red one,'" he says. "Buy that and the fund gets $20." Red is only a "win-win-win," he notes, if it drives higher sales for the store or manufacturer. "The premise is, you will sell more with this logo. If you sell the same amount it won't work. They're not

Distracting and Compromising

Consumption philanthropy individualizes solutions to collective social problems, distracting our attention and resources away from the neediest causes, the most effective interventions, and the act of critical questioning itself. It devalues the moral core of philanthropy by making virtuous action easy and thoughtless. And it obscures the links between markets—their firms, products, and services—and the negative impacts they can have on human well-being. For these reasons, consumption philanthropy compromises the potential for charity to better society.

Angela M. Eikenberry,
"The Hidden Costs of Cause Marketing,"
Standard Social Innovation Review, *Summer 2009.*

in business to give away a piece of their margin. They're in business to give away that residual piece of their margin that comes from Red."

His goal is to build a brand, he says, not create an efficient way to give to AIDS in Africa. (That said, Red has earmarked funds [to] be spent on "women and children" because programs devoted to treatment and education of girls and women deliver the greatest return on investment.) "My job is to make Red a well-known-enough brand so that 10 years from now people will think of it like the Nike swoosh. I want to create a brand marketers feel they must have or they will lose business." Given that each vendor handles its own design, maintaining brand integrity is a challenge; all products and marketing imagery are vetted through Red. Shriver calls the *Advertising Age*'s story "criminally negligent." He's in talks with prospective Red vendors. If they pass, he won't know whether or not the fallout was a factor. Red has donated more money to AIDS in Africa than Ireland, Saudi Arabia, even China, Shriver notes. "Instead of slamming Bono, *Ad Age* should slam China." As for donating directly, he's for it. "I think it's thrilling if it would happen in the real world," he says. "But I wonder if any of those guys who set up the Web site had ever donated to the Global Fund or even heard of it prior to Red."

Periodical Bibliography

The following articles have been selected to supplement the diverse views presented in this chapter.

Danny Duncan Collum	"This Ad Is Your Ad," *Sojourners*, February 2007.
Sophia Dembling	"Mixed Messages," *Scouting*, October 2008.
Angela M. Eikenberry	"The Hidden Costs of Cause Marketing," *Stanford Social Innovation Review*, Summer 2009.
Sean Gregory	"Are Direct-to-Consumer Drug Ads Doomed?" *TIME*, February 4, 2009.
Lorraine Duffy Merkl	"Dumb and Dumber: Ads That Make Men Look Bad Don't Help Women Either," *Adweek*, March 19, 2007.
Cahal Milmo	"Advertising Stereotypes: From the Kitchen to First Class," *Independent* (United Kingdom), June 17, 2005.
Dan Neil	"Government Can't Ban Drug Advertising, but It Can Take the Life Out of the Ads," *Los Angeles Times*, July 14, 2009.
Gary Ruskin and Juliet Schor	"Every Nook and Cranny: The Dangerous Spread of Commercialized Culture," *Multinational Monitor*, January-February 2005.

OPPOSING
VIEWPOINTS®
SERIES

CHAPTER 2

Does Advertising Exploit Children?

Chapter Preface

In October 2009, the Nutrition Council of Oregon kicked off a statewide campaign against junk food advertising that targets children. It includes ads in two hundred buses and child and health care services as well as a Facebook page. The typical American child sees forty thousand ads a year, according to Jennifer Young of the Office of Family Health at Oregon's Public Health Division. "Half of those ads are for food," she contends, "and 97 percent of those are for sugared cereal, high-calorie snacks and fast food."[1]

Advocates argue that such ads are linked to growing rates of childhood obesity, which have risen globally and tripled in the United States since 1984. "We know that advertising has a part to play in shaping children's diets and that TV is the principal medium for food advertising,"[2] maintains Peter Kopelman of the Royal College of Physicians in London. Moreover, a 2008 study by the National Bureau of Economic Research (NBER) claims that banning fast-food commercials could trim down the number of overweight American children by 18 percent. "We have known for some time that childhood obesity has gripped our culture, but little empirical research has been done that identifies television advertising as a possible cause," states Shin-Yi Chou, an economist who participated in the study. "Hopefully, this line of research can lead to a serious discussion about the type of policies that can curb America's obesity epidemic."[3]

Nevertheless, other commentators believe that childhood obesity must be addressed in other ways. "A big part of the problem is that many children have very few options after school to do anything other than sit in front of television or computer screens or hang out on their neighborhood streets," proposes Carol Glazer, program and policy consultant for the After School Project. "Can we offer them choices that will help them stay safe and physically active, as well as learn social skills and build self-confidence?"[4] In the following chapter, the authors examine the effects of advertising on child consumers.

Notes

1. *Portlander*, October 14, 2009. http://theportlander.com.
2. *Mail Online*, June 9, 2006. www.dailymail.co.uk.
3. Reuters, November 20, 2008. www.reuters.com.
4. *Boston Globe*, September 5, 2005. www.boston.com.

> *"The commercialization of childhood threatens children of their right to develop to their full potential as social beings—a most basic right of childhood."*

Advertising Is Harmful to Children

Diane E. Levin

Diane E. Levin is an education professor at Wheelock College in Boston, Massachusetts, and cofounder of "Campaign for a Commercial-Free Childhood." In the following viewpoint, Levin writes that advertising has negative effects on children. Aggressive marketing imbues young consumers with materialistic values, and toys and media linked to popular entertainment deprive them of creative thinking and learning, she argues. Levin upholds that ads and media messages reinforce stereotypical gender roles for boys and girls, hindering healthy, positive social interactions with their peers. She recommends that parents counteract the influence of a commercial-saturated culture by limiting its exposure to children.

Diane E. Levin, "Too Young to Be a Consumer: The Toll of Commercial Culture on the Rights of Childhood," *Exchange*, May-June 2009, pp. 49–54. Reproduced by permission.

As you read, consider the following questions:

1. How do best-selling commercial toys limit children's play, in Diane E. Levin's opinion?

2. How does the "quick fix to happiness" of buying new products affect children, in the author's view?

3. What gender roles and behaviors do girls and boys learn from commercial culture, as stated by the author?

A preschool teacher reports, "My student, Gabe, who talks about Batman and the Power Rangers all day dissolved into tears when we were out of masking tape and he couldn't figure out how to make himself a 'power shooter' bracelet. Gabe cried, 'Then I won't have powers!' It seemed his prop was critical for him to be happy and know how to play. He often comments that school is no fun because we don't have the right toys, i.e., those he has at home that are directly linked to the Batman and Power Ranger movies."

When parents arrive to pick up their five-year-old daughters from a birthday party, they are surprised to find that they all have heavy makeup on. Music from the Disney movie, *HS Musical 3* [*High School Musical 3: Senior Year*], is blaring and the girls are doing a hip-gyrating, sexy dance taught to them by the birthday girl's teenage cousin. At a store the next day, one party attendee, Jessica, runs to a *HS Musical* padded bra and bikini panty set and excitedly demands that her mother buy it for her—another girl at the party just got them! Every time a lively rhythm comes on the PA [public address] system, Jessica begins gyrating her hips just like on the screen. She practices her dancing at home, too, and keeps asking to see the movie.

A parent worriedly wrote me about her first-grade son, Julian. He and two of his friends have just been sent to the principal's office for the third time in as many weeks for attacking another child on the playground. They play 'good guys' and randomly label an unsuspecting child on the playground the 'bad guy.' Then they attack him just like in their 'favorite' superhero movie.

Four-year-olds unable to play without special Batman shooters! Five-year-olds wanting bras and bikini underwear so they can be like teenage movie stars! Six-year-olds regularly being sent to the principal for attacking unsuspecting classmates! What's going on? Are these stories that would have occurred 25 years ago? What do they say about children and childhood of today? Should we be concerned? And what can we do about it?

What's Going on Today?

The culture in which children grow up—what they see and hear in the world around them—has a huge impact on their likes and dislikes, how they treat each other, their ideas about how the world works and what will make them happy and fulfilled, and even how likely they are to reach their full potential as individuals. The above stories provide a window into the experiences the media and commercial culture that surrounds children today. They can teach us a lot about what children are learning and even how it may be depriving them of the childhoods they need to develop their full potential.

Screens, Screens Everywhere! Today, screens are a major force in children's lives. There are screens in bedrooms, kitchens, minivans, airports, and shopping malls. What's going on as children sit in front of a screen?

- They are having secondhand experiences—not directly involved in the real world having the concrete hands-on experiences we know are so important for their development and learning.

- They are learning someone else's lessons—i.e., the scriptwriter's—about who are the good and bad guys and what good and bad guys do, about the clothes they need to buy to be pretty and 'cool' and how they should act when they're wearing those clothes, i.e., sexy clothes for sexy dances. These are often not the lessons the people who care about them are trying to teach.

- They are getting used to the frenetic, high-intensity zap, zap stimulation that can make everything else seem boring when the screen is turned off.

- They are not exploring their own ideas, working out their own solutions to problems, being creative and imaginative in their own unique ways, but rather are being programmed by someone else.

Marketing Madness! Children live in a world of marketing without borders. Marketers do not necessarily have the best interests of children in mind when they market to children; rather, their job is to try to capture children's attention so they will want to buy a product. Their job is to get children to want their products—more and more, never enough, promising happiness, brand loyalty at younger and younger ages. In fact, companies spend approximately $17 billion annually marketing to children, an increase from about $1,000 in 1983. In 1984 the Federal Communications Commission [FCC] deregulated children's television and it became possible to market products to children through television programming for the first time. How has this media-marketing onslaught affected children? Today, children live in a world where:

- Between the ages of 2 and 11 years old, children see more than 25,000 advertisements a year on television alone.

- From *Star Wars*, *The Incredible Hulk*, and *Spider-Man* action figures to Bratz dolls and Disney Princesses, most of today's best-selling toys are linked to screens— television, movies, computer games, and Web sites.

Red and Rover used with the permission of Brian Basset and the Washington Post Writers Group in conjunction with the Cartoonist Group.

These toys, that are replicas of what is seen on the screen, tell children that when they play they should use the toys to imitate what they saw on the screen, not create their own imaginative play. The backs of toy boxes have pictures of all the other toys children can get in the toy line and children know there are always more to want.

- From morning to night, children are assaulted by products with logos linked to the media—on breakfast cereal boxes and lunch boxes, bedsheets and pajamas, tee shirts and underwear—keeping media images and the products associated with them on children's minds all the time.

- The quick fix to happiness often means that getting some new sought-after product brings children more happiness than using what was received. Or the happiness that comes from using what was received quickly wears off as something new in an ad or that their friend has captures their attention.

- Parenting is harder as there are more and more things parents have to say "no" to, creating stress and driving a wedge between parents and children as children often feel parents' "nos" are depriving them of their quick fix happiness.

The Price Children Pay

The stories at the beginning of this article illustrate a few of the ways media and commercial culture [are] affecting children's behavior. But more than that, they point to how children's basic right to develop their full potential—socially, emotionally, and intellectually—is being assaulted and undermined.

Bye, Bye Play. Screen time and highly realistic, media-linked toys are depriving children of the creative play they need for their optimal development and well-being. We see this in all three of the stories above. Jessica's 'play' is imitating the sexy dancing in *High School Musical*. Gabe is obsessed with Batman and Power Rangers and doesn't like the open-ended toys that allow for more creative play at school. He is brought to tears when he can't make the prop he needs to replicate what his favorite media character uses. If he can't have the proper toys, then he can't play. And Julian is so intent on imitating the good guy on the screen who attacks bad guys, that he seems to abandon all he knows about caring social behavior and either doesn't care about or doesn't think in advance about the punishment he will receive.

All three of these children focus their energy on imitating favorite television characters whom they know from second-hand experience. They are not using their creativity and imagination to develop their own characters and scripts, problems and solutions from their direct experience. They have a hard time coming up with their own interesting and meaningful problems to work on and solve in their own unique ways—the very foundation of learning, development, and well-being. In a sense, it seems like these children are remote controlled by forces that have power over them, rather than being independent, resourceful, and meaningfully engaged players. It also feels like they have developed Problem Solving Deficit Disorder (PSDD), the inability to find and solve interesting problems that are at the heart of play and learning.

When children do not engage regularly in creative play, their optimal development and learning is undermined. They are more likely to have short attention spans, flit from thing to thing, and be at loose ends when they have free time or during 'free play'. This is one of the most compelling reasons why media and marketing forces in the lives of children today are undermining and threatening children's basic right to develop their full potential.

Tough Boys, Sexy Girls. In caring environments, through give-and-take interactions with others, children gradually learn how to have positive and respectful relationships and how to work out problems with others in a peaceful manner. If the environment doesn't give children opportunities to interact and model mean-spirited or dehumanized interactions, the opposite is likely to happen.

What social lessons are the children learning in the three stories above? Gabe is so caught up in having the right superhero prop that he doesn't seem to be interested in or able to play with other children during playtime. Social interactions seem secondary to imitating a script. As Jessica gets caught up in the desire to become involved with the media, products, and behavior connected to her exposure to *High School Musical*, stress is put on her relationship with her mother. And Julian seems to shut out or be impervious to the impact of his actions on others—hurting some anonymous child—as imitating the tough, aggressive behavior he sees on the screen takes precedence.

Today, screen time takes time away from interacting, and thereby learning how to interact, with other children. This means that many children have fewer opportunities to learn positive social behavior. In addition, as children are glued to the screen, the messages designed to get them to buy things teach lessons that undermine positive social behavior. Girls learn to judge themselves and other girls as objects—how they look and what they can buy determines their value, not what they can actually do; boys learn to judge girls this way too. And boys learn to judge themselves and other boys by how strong, independent, and ready to fight they are.

These messages are promoting extreme gender stereotypes that narrow the options for what both girls and boys can be and do. They are also turning both girls and boys into objects, who are judged by how well they meet the stereotypes. It's much easier to be mean and uncaring to an object than to a person. This can lead to what often feels like compassion deficit disorder (CDD)—children not knowing how to have caring, connected, give-and-take relationships and more likely to bully and tease each other. The commercialization of childhood threatens children of their right to develop to their full potential as social beings—a most basic right of childhood.

Reclaiming Childhood

Children urgently need the important grown-ups in their lives to help them counteract the harm caused to their childhoods by commercialization. Here is what a comprehensive and meaningful response, directed at children, families, schools, communities, and the wider society, might be:

- Protect children as much as possible from exposure to commercial culture. Help parents create rules and routines around media use as well as what is purchased, when, and how.

- Restore children's right to develop their full potential through play by helping them:

    Regain control of their play so it is not remote controlled;

    Find deeply meaningful content to bring to their play that comes from direct experience, not the screen;

    Become good problem finders and problem solvers in their play in order to counteract PSDD;

Find interesting problems to work on and develop the skills needed to solve them;

Have large blocks of uninterrupted time when they can play at home and school;

Learn to use open-ended materials such as play dough or blocks in the service of their play, rather than toys that control the play.

- Help counteract the harmful lessons children are learning from commercialized childhood, including narrow gender stereotypes and compassion deficit disorder. Work to:

    Establish safe channels of communication, whereby children know they can talk to a trusted adult about what they see, hear, think and are worried about without being embarrassed, ridiculed or punished;

    Reduce gender stereotypes. Help boys and girls expand their concepts of what is okay for them to do as boys and girls and develop a broad range of interests, skills, and behaviors;

    Help children develop caring relationships and find positive ways to solve problems and conflicts with each other;

    Teach alternative lessons to the mean spirited, sexist and violent messages taught by commercial culture;

    Help children find the deep satisfaction that comes from solving problems and mastering new skills—so they learn "I can do it!" instead of "I want it!"

    Parents and schools need to work together to support children's right to childhood.

Work at all levels to create a society that is more supportive of children's healthy gender and sexual development. This includes promoting public policies that reduce the sexualization of children and limiting the power of corporations to market sex to children.

| *"These advertising fears feed on this stunted, oversimplified view of children's knowledge and abilities."*

The Fears of Advertising's Effects on Children Are Exaggerated

Karen Sternheimer

Karen Sternheimer is a lecturer in the Department of Sociology at the University of Southern California and author of It's Not the Media: The Truth About Pop Culture's Influence on Children. *In the following viewpoint, excerpted from her book, Sternheimer maintains that fears about advertising and youth underestimate what children and adolescents know and the capabilities they possess. Advertisers attempt to appeal to the concerns and desires of childhood, she asserts, such as the constraints of adult authority and fitting in with peers, which parents may find objectionable or worrisome. Rather than blame advertising, the author recommends it be used to understand adults' relationships with children and consumerism.*

As you read, consider the following questions:

1. Name the two countries banning advertising aimed at children under twelve.

2. What do fears of advertising reflect about adults, in Karen Sternheimer's opinion?

3. How does Sternheimer support her position that children are not easily persuaded by ads to want a product?

There is no shortage of people who believe advertisers have an unfair advantage over children, as a variety of news reports reveal. A spring 2000 *USA Today* article reported that psychologists have considered sanctioning colleagues who consult with advertisers. A *Boston Herald* story described an advocacy group called Stop Commercial Exploitation of Children, which calls for the federal government to create new regulations like those in Norway and Sweden, which ban advertisements targeted at children under twelve. The group describes advertising as "a $12.8 billion-a-year industry that targets society's most vulnerable minds and deliberately excludes parents." Articles in the *Nation* and the *American Prospect* describe children as "exploited" by marketers and in need of government protection because they are vulnerable to "being programmed" and are "too young to understand . . . that advertising may be harmful."

Advertising is frequently described by its detractors as "emotionally harmful" to children, created by "corporate exploiters of children." During her campaign for the Senate, Hillary Rodham Clinton called for limits on "advertising that is harmful to children," which begs the question: When is advertising "harmful?" Are we living [in] "a toxic cultural environment," as author Jean Kilbourne says, created by advertising? Harm is rather loosely defined. For some, the fact that teenagers can easily identify brands of beer from advertisements is cause for alarm. The concept of danger is difficult to empirically demonstrate but is instead described anecdotally to support demands that advertising is a clear hazard to children. Children are threatened, the logic goes, and therefore some adults ask the government (or have anointed themselves) to protect children from allegedly all-powerful advertisers. Kids are often targets of aggressive marketing campaigns, and this creates worry and anger.

Fear of advertising is peppered with language of assault and exploitation of a wide-eyed, simple-minded unsuspecting child. Children are presumed helpless in the face of advertising, described as "sacrificed for corporate profit" by manipulative, greedy Madison Avenue [New York City street that is synonymous with the advertising industry] executives. Parents are encouraged to "combat the effects of advertisements" and protect their children. There's a big problem with this line of thinking, and it stems from the sentimentalized caricature of children and childhood. These advertising fears feed on this stunted, oversimplified view of children's knowledge and abilities. Of course young people (and adults) can be influenced by advertising campaigns and enjoy partaking in consumer culture. But before we assume children are always naïve consumers, it would be wise to find out what children already know, what capabilities and limitations they possess. We can work to create competency in dealing with advertising, but instead we often struggle to maintain the belief that children are weak and in need of protection. Competency building threatens the power adults hold over children and is seldom the focus of advertising fears.

A Challenge to Parental Boundaries

Advertising does represent a challenge to parental boundaries. Advertisers don't ask parents' permission to speak with their children; they bypass parents and tell kids about things parents sometimes don't want them to know about, like candy and sugary cereals. The fact that children are a viable target market upsets many adults because it reminds us that children's influences have expanded beyond their parents alone, and that television is a major part of childhood. A *Los Angeles Times* article noted that "parents face (competition) in shaping their children's values," which is certainly true, but advertising and mass media are by no means the only competing factors when we consider the influence of peers, teachers, and other adults. Fears of the "danger" of advertising reveal adult anxieties about being unable to control children's interests and identities, which are in part demonstrated through consumption. Adult concerns about the nature of our consumption-driven society are more easily deflected onto children, because it's easier to worry about someone else's material desires than to question our own. Parents are charged with the responsibility of teaching kids how to be responsible consumers, which can feel overwhelming.

But while many adults jump to conclusions about what children can and can't understand, advertisers' use of research enables them to have a better understanding of central issues important to young people. In fact, advertisers describe marketing to children as a bigger challenge than selling to adults. By talking with kids within market research, advertisers learn about the power struggles many children feel between themselves and their parents and reflect this back in their ad campaigns. Marketers see young people of all ages trying to create separate identities from their parents, and thus food, toys, and fashion are all marketed as ways to be distinct from adults, yet similar to their friends. Public discussions describing young people as incapable of making informed decisions enhance the tensions they feel toward adults. Of course, advertisers are certainly not child advocates, and only attempt to address these feelings in order to sell things. The imbalance of power, as well as the desire to feel grown up, to be independent yet part of the crowd, are real elements of children's lives that many adults overlook when focusing only on children's shortcomings as consumers.

The End of Kids' TV?

Getting rid of adverts [advertisements] aimed at children means that kids' media simply won't be made in the future. From Web sites to TV shows, most of the media [rely] on advertising for [their] funding. Take away advertisers' cash and you remove the reason the content was created in the first place.

KidsandAdvertising,
"Could Advertising Be Good for Kids?"
www.kidsandadvertising.co.uk.

What Advertisers Know

Advertisers spend a great deal of their financial resources studying their target markets and learning about their values, beliefs, and their lifestyles. They are some of the only people who want to learn about children's fantasies and beliefs before making decisions about them. I am certainly not suggesting we celebrate market research departments because they listen to children; their main interest lies in co-opting youth culture and transforming it into a commodity, and the information they gather is not used to improve children's lives in a serious sort of way. Nonetheless, advertisers cannot afford to make assumptions about children like many of us do; there is simply too much money at stake.

So how do advertisers know what they know? They rely on research in the form of surveys with older groups, but more often than not researchers become anthropologists of "kid culture." This is accomplished through the use of methods like focus groups, where a group of about a dozen is selected from the targeted age range and meets to answer a facilitator's questions. A good facilitator puts aside the role of omniscient adult long enough to let the young participants become the experts and inform the researchers about specific trends and their opinions about a product or other more general issues. As an episode of PBS's *FRONTLINE* titled "The Merchants of Cool" detailed, marketers are constantly struggling to pin down what is currently "cool," something constantly shifting. To discover the mystery of "cool," researchers rely on "cool consultants," or a panel of fashion-forward young people who report on trends within their peer groups for a fee. Very young (or young-looking) marketing staffers sometimes go out in the field themselves to mingle with teens to spy on them and co-opt any new trends. Of course the preeminent goal is selling a product, but marketing research is one of the few instances where adults treat kids as the experts of their own culture, and offer a chance for them to be heard (and paid).

Based on their research, advertisers create ads that they think will reflect central concerns that will resonate with their audience, be they children or adults. Marketing executives make a priority of finding out what kids in their target demographic are most concerned with. Sociologist Michael Schudson explains that "advertisements pick up and represent values already in the culture . . . [and] pick up some of the things that people hold dear and re-present them . . . assuring them that the sponsor is the patron of common ideals." Advertisements for children thus appear to be sympathetic to kids and at times critical of adults. They mirror back whatever the target market wants to hear, and this message is clearly threatening to adults.

Here's what market researchers have found: Not surprisingly, children often long for freedom and independence and feel constrained by adult authority while still wanting to know that they will be loved and cared for. Jane Hobson, associate director of Research International, notes, "The trick is to aim a product just high enough so that older kids pick up on it and then it can filter down." Jane Mathews, a British advertising specialist, similarly reports, "Children want to seem older and in control in an adult world . . . and they want to be accepted by their friends." In fact, peers are more important sources of information for young people than advertising and influence their purchases more directly. Teens are also less likely to watch television than adults, particularly if they are from affluent families.

But simply understanding a target group's central concerns doesn't guarantee sales. In fact, an ad campaign is considered successful not simply based on sales but on whether brand awareness and market share increase. Advertising has been relatively unsuccessful in changing the size of a market and is instead most effective in obtaining a larger market share of those *already* consuming a product. If we consumers have an image to associate with a product, it may make us more likely to choose one particular brand over another, yet research demonstrates that brand awareness does not necessarily lead to acceptance of a product or a purchase. This does not mean that advertising is unimportant or inconsequential. On the contrary, it reveals a great deal about relevant issues within American society. But advertising doesn't work the way many of us think it does. Commercials don't necessarily make anyone—child or otherwise—immediately think "I have to have that." Instead, advertising often works to remind us of a brand name and to link a particular image with their product. That's why most of us would feel more comfortable brushing our teeth with Crest toothpaste than a generic tube. We think we know something about Crest, based on experience and from advertising.

Even liking an ad doesn't mean a child will want a product. For instance, an article in *Marketing*, a British trade magazine, described a ten-year-old boy who loves a yogurt commercial yet says he dislikes yogurt and does not plan on eating any. The report went on to note that children are often entertained by ads, but this does not mean they are interested in the product. So children, like adults, arc not necessarily tricked into buying things by slick ads that they may enjoy. Consumer behavior is more complex than cause-effect; persuasion is multifaceted and advertising is merely part of this process.

Not Gullible Targets

And advertisers know this. "They may be young, but they're not dumb," wrote Kristina Feliciano in *Mediaweek*, an American trade magazine. "Kids don't want to be spoken down to, and they know from 'lame,'" she warned advertisers. This information shouldn't come as a big surprise, but it is indicative of advertisers' attempts to understand children from their own perspective, rather than consider children as simply less competent than adults. Jane Mathews, the British advertising specialist, reminds her colleagues that ads that seem patronizing to children do not work. A marketing textbook offers similar "timeless rules" of advertising to the youth market: Never talk down to youth, be totally straightforward, and treat youth as if they are rational, thinking people. Too bad when we adults complain about children's incompetence we don't realize these simple truths.

Unlike most adults, advertisers do not consider their young targets particularly gullible. "If there were a magic formula, we'd all be rich," an ad executive reports. Instead, trade publications often speak of children as especially skeptical and difficult to address. *Marketing* writer Patrick Barrett notes that children are not necessarily "a gullible soft target, but in fact are hard to hit and quick to switch off . . . ad messages."

Advertisers are fully aware of the knowledge they possess that other adults, particularly parents, do not when it comes to understanding children. Marketing executive Andrew Marsden finds kids skeptical and knowledgeable about the communications world, and noted that children are often more independent than their parents are willing to admit. "There is an element of naïveté from parents. The world they grew up in no longer exists," he remarked in *Campaign*, a marketing trade magazine. He also finds teenagers to be particularly good at manipulating parents. In spite of the popular (and tautological) belief that advertising must be highly effective since so much money is spent doing it, advertisers are not overly confident about their ability to reach young target markets. In fact, because children are seen as a challenge, some companies such as Burger King have hired specialized agencies to handle their children's campaign. It seems it may be easier to influence the parents.

What advertisers know is not earth-shattering. It is not surprising to learn that young people are interested in connecting with peers, that popular culture is important, and so is the chance to feel heard in an adult-centered world. These ideas surface throughout advertisements created for young people. Instead of focusing on advertising's influence, we can use it to learn about our relationship with both children and consumption rather than only blaming media for kids' consumer behavior.

> "There is an ongoing need . . . for alcohol companies to adopt a more meaningful and effective standard for where they place their advertisements."

Children Are Overexposed to Alcohol Advertising

David Jernigan

David Jernigan is executive director of the Center on Alcohol Marketing and Youth (CAMY) and associate professor at Bloomberg School of Public Health at Johns Hopkins University. Children and adolescents continue to be exposed to advertisements for alcohol, writes Jernigan in the following viewpoint, influencing underage drinking and increasing the likelihood of alcoholism later in life. While such advertising is declining in magazines and public television, he declares that placements for liquor on cable television have skyrocketed and account for 95 percent of youth exposure to such ads. Jernigan recommends that the industry tighten its self-regulatory marketing standards to help protect young audiences.

David Jernigan, "Intoxicating Brands: Alcohol Advertising and Youth," *Multinational Monitor*, July-August 2008. Ratings and other data contained herein are © Nielsen Media Research, Inc. All rights reserved. Reproduced by permission.

As you read, consider the following questions:

1. How does David Jernigan back his argument that underage drinking leads to future alcohol abuse?

2. According to the author, which brands are the least effective at limiting youth exposure to alcohol ads?

3. How much more likely were youth to see alcohol ads that emphasize responsibility as compared to regular alcohol ads?

People were drinking alcohol long before the alcohol industry hooked up with Madison Avenue [New York City street that is synonymous with the advertising industry], but the beer, wine and liquor companies clearly believe advertising affects consumption patterns.

Alcohol companies spend close to $2 billion every year advertising in the United States alone. From 2001 to 2007, they aired more than 2 million television ads and published more than 20,000 magazine advertisements.

Such heavy advertising inevitably leads to heavy youth exposure. That so much of the industry's advertising is aired on programming, or published in magazines, with large youth audiences makes this problem much worse.

From 2001 to 2007, youth exposure to alcohol product advertising on television rose by 38 percent. The average number of television advertisements seen in a year by youth increased from 216 to 301.

In 2007, approximately one out of every five alcohol product advertisements on television was on programming that youth ages 12 to 20 were more likely per capita to see than adults of the legal drinking age. Almost all of them were on cable television, where distilled spirits companies in particular have dramatically increased their alcohol advertising in the past seven years. This large and increasing TV exposure offset reductions in magazine exposure over the same time period.

The data comes from researchers with the Center on Alcohol Marketing and Youth (CAMY) at Georgetown University and Virtual Media Resources (VMR) of Natick, Massachusetts, who analyzed the placements of 2,033,931 alcohol product advertisements that aired on television between 2001 and 2007, and 19,466 alcohol advertisements placed in national magazines between 2001 and 2006.

All of this advertising—and other industry marketing strategies—matters. Heavier youth exposure to advertising leads to more alcohol consumption, researchers have found. Alcohol use and abuse takes a serious, direct toll on youth in deaths, injuries, academic performance and emotional well-being, and earlier and heavier drinking sets up kids for worse health outcomes later in life.

Fueling Underage Drinking

Alcohol is the leading drug problem among young people. According to *Monitoring the Future*, the federal government's annual survey of drug use among eighth-, 10th- and 12th-graders, more young people drink alcohol than smoke cigarettes or use illegal drugs. The U.S. Surgeon General estimates that approximately 5,000 people under age 21 die from alcohol-related injuries involving underage drinking each year.

Despite significant efforts to reduce youth access to alcohol, binge drinking among youth remains stubbornly high. In 2006, 7.2 million youth under age 21 reported binge drinking (consuming five or more drinks at a sitting, usually defined as within two hours) within the past month.

The earlier young people start drinking, the worse the consequences. People who start drinking before age 15 are four times more likely to become dependent on alcohol later in life than those who wait to drink until they are 21. Those who drink heavily in adolescence and early adulthood are more likely to develop a metabolic profile that puts them at greater risk of cardiovascular problems later in life, whether or not they continue drinking.

"Too many Americans consider underage drinking a rite of passage to adulthood," says former Acting Surgeon General Kenneth Moritsugu. "Research shows that young people who start drinking before the age of 15 are five times more likely to have alcohol-related problems later in life. New research also indicates that alcohol may harm the developing adolescent brain. The availability of this research provides more reasons than ever before for parents and other adults to protect the health and safety of our nation's children."

There is compelling evidence that exposure to alcohol advertising and marketing increases the likelihood of underage drinking. Since 2001, at least seven peer-reviewed, federally funded, long-term studies have found that young people with greater exposure to alcohol marketing—including on television, in magazines, on the radio, on billboards or other outdoor signage, or via in-store beer displays, beer concessions, or ownership of beer promotional items or branded merchandise—are more likely to start drinking than their peers.

Econometric analysis based on data from youth drinking surveys has estimated that a 28 percent reduction in alcohol advertising would reduce the percentage of adolescents who drank in the last month by 4 to 16 percent. The percentage engaging in binge drinking monthly would fall by 8 to 33 percent.

Alcohol Advertising Tsunami

Between 2001 and 2007, alcohol companies spent $6.6 billion to place more than 2 million alcohol product advertisements on television. From 2001 to 2006, they spent $2 billion to place 19,466 alcohol product advertisements in national magazines.

Because the four broadcast networks—NBC, CBS, ABC and FOX—have a voluntary ban on distilled spirits advertising on television, beer companies have traditionally dominated spending on television. However, since 2001, distilled spirits marketers have driven a dramatic increase in alcohol advertising on cable television.

Advertising placements, spending and youth exposure have all grown on television since 2001, while placements and youth exposure have declined in magazines. The number of magazine advertisements placed by alcohol companies fell by 22 percent from 2001 to 2006. Spending in magazines peaked at $361 million in 2004 but fell to $331 million in 2006. Youth, young adult and adult exposure to this advertising fell by 50 percent, 33 percent and 28 percent respectively over the six-year period. Overall, the shift from magazines to television means that there has been little change in overall youth exposure to alcohol advertising across the two media since 2001.

Exposing Kids

In 2003, trade associations for beer and distilled spirits companies adopted, as part of their self-regulatory codes of good marketing practice, a 30 percent maximum for underage audiences of their advertising (the wine industry had moved to 30 percent in 2000). Under this standard, alcohol companies should not advertise on programs with an audience that is more than 30 percent underage.

In the same year that the beer and spirits industries adopted the 30 percent standard, the National Research Council [NRC] and Institute of Medicine [IOM] recommended that alcohol companies move toward a proportional 15 percent maximum for youth audiences of alcohol advertising, since 12- to 20-year-olds are roughly 15 percent of the general population. In 2006, 20 state attorneys general echoed that call, followed by the U.S. Surgeon General in 2007.

Even a 15 percent standard would leave large numbers of kids exposed to alcohol ads. A program with high ratings but a relatively lower proportion of youth viewers may still reach more kids than a program with a higher proportion of youth viewers but a smaller overall audience.

Since adopting the 30 percent standard in 2003, alcohol companies have made steady progress toward compliance, both in magazines and on television. In 2001, 11 percent of alcohol product advertisements in magazines were in publications with youth readership greater than 30 percent. By 2006, only 3 percent of alcohol product advertisements in magazines were in publications with youth readerships greater than 30 percent.

On television, in 2001, 11 percent of alcohol product advertisements were on television programming with youth audiences greater than 30 percent. By 2007, 6 percent of alcohol product advertisements were on television programming with youth audiences greater than 30 percent.

However, the decline in placements on television programming with youth audiences greater than 30 percent has been accompanied by increases in the percent of youth exposure coming from overexposing placements—ads on programs with 15 to 30 percent youth viewership. Youth overexposure occurs when advertising is placed on programming or in publications with youth audiences that are out of proportion to their presence in the population. Cable generated 95 percent of youth overexposure to alcohol advertising on television in 2007.

The result is that the share of youth exposure to alcohol advertising coming from advertisements on television programming that youth are more likely per capita to watch than adults has never been higher since CAMY began its monitoring in 2001. More than 40 percent of total youth exposure to alcohol ads on TV comes from programs where 12- to 20-year-olds are more than 15 percent of the audience.

Oriented Toward Youth

The introduction of cartoon or animal characters further attempts to attract young viewers to alcohol. In recent commercials, alcohol advertisers have used frogs, lizards and dogs, which were overwhelmingly admired by youth. In 1996, for example, the Budweiser Frogs were more recognizable to children aged 9–11 than the Power Rangers, Tony the Tiger, or Smokey the Bear. Many alcohol advertisements use other techniques oriented toward youth, such as themes of rebellion and use of adolescent humor.

American Academy of Family Physicians,
"Alcohol Advertising and Youth," 2004. www.aafp.org.

The Overexposers

Not all alcohol brands advertise equally. A relative handful of brands are responsible for nearly half of all youth overexposure to alcohol ads.

In magazines in 2006, 21 alcohol brands (out of a total of 229 alcohol brands advertising in magazines) were responsible for 44 percent of youth exposure and 49 percent of youth overexposure, but only 33 percent of adult exposure to alcohol product advertising.

On television in 2006, 22 alcohol brands (out of a total of 142 alcohol brands advertising on television) provided 36 percent of youth exposure and 48 percent of youth overexposure but only 30 percent of adult exposure to alcohol product advertising.

Clearly some brands do better than others at avoiding youth overexposure. Using 2007 television data, CAMY developed a method for identifying which brands did best overall both in complying with the industry's 30 percent threshold and in avoiding youth overexposure to alcohol advertising. Eliminating the smallest brands to avoid skewing the results, 11 brands stood out as the worst performers and seven brands emerged as best.

The worst performers were: Miller Lite, Corona Extra beer, Coors Light, Hennessy Cognacs, Guinness beers, Samuel Adams beers, Bud Light, Smirnoff vodkas, Disaronno Originale Amaretto, Miller Chill and multiple brands from Mike's beverages.

The best performers by the CAMY measure were: Michelob beer, Santa Margherita Pinot Grigio, Korbel California Champagne, Arbor Mist wines, Rolling Rock beer, Michelob Ultra Light beer and Kahlúa Hazelnut.

Not Too Much Responsibility

In addition to placing product advertising on television, some alcohol companies also place "responsibility" advertisements, which seek to deliver messages about underage drinking or about drinking safely (i.e., in moderation, not in combination with driving, and so on).

From 2001 to 2007, alcohol companies spent 43 times as much money to place 28 times as many product advertisements as "responsibility" messages.

Placement of this kind of advertising varies by company. Diageo, the world's largest distilled spirits company and marketer of Smirnoff vodkas and Captain Morgan rums, spent nearly 19 percent of its television advertising dollars on "responsibility" messages from 2001 to 2007. In contrast, Anheuser-Busch, producer of Budweiser and Bud Light and the largest alcohol advertiser on television, spent 1 percent of its budget on these messages (and in total dollars, less than a quarter of what Diageo spent).

Youth and adult exposure to the alcohol industry's "responsibility" messages has consistently been overwhelmed by the amount of alcohol product advertising seen by each group each year. From 2001 to 2007, youth ages 12 to 20 were 22 times more likely to see a product advertisement for alcohol than an alcohol industry–funded "responsibility" message. Adults were 26 times more likely to see an alcohol product advertisement than an alcohol industry–funded "responsibility" message.

The Path to Reform

Over the last decade, the alcohol industry has tightened and clarified its self-regulatory standards and review procedures. However, although alcohol industry compliance with the voluntary 30 percent maximum for youth audiences of alcohol advertising has been good, this threshold has not been effective in reducing youth exposure to alcohol advertising. Youth exposure to alcohol advertising in magazines has fallen, but this has been counteracted by the huge increase in alcohol advertising on television, especially in distilled spirits advertising on cable television.

During this same period, federally funded surveys have found that binge-drinking 12th-grade girls (the only grade for which data are available) have shifted their beverage of choice from beer to liquor since 2001, and that in four states (the only places from which data are available), current drinkers in grades nine through 12 are also now more likely to drink liquor.

Nearly half of youth overexposure to alcohol advertising on television and in magazines results from placements by a small number of brands, suggesting that the majority of the industry is able to advertise its products without overexposing youth. The U.S. Surgeon General has stated that alcohol companies have a public responsibility to ensure that the placement of their advertising does not disproportionately expose youth to messages about alcohol.

In 2006, Congress passed unanimously—and [former] president George W. Bush signed into law—legislation authorizing the Department of Health and Human Services to monitor and report annually to Congress the "rate of exposure of youth to advertising and other media messages encouraging and discouraging alcohol consumption." To date, however, no funds have been appropriated for this activity, and no such reporting has occurred.

The prevalence and the toll of underage drinking in the United States remain high. Evidence that alcohol advertising plays a role in the problem grows stronger each year. With approximately 5,000 young lives per year in the United States at stake, there is an ongoing need not only for independent monitoring, but also for alcohol companies to adopt a more meaningful and effective standard for where they place their advertisements.

On cable television, the industry's 30 percent standard leaves 82 percent of advertising time slots available for alcohol advertising. The standard has not succeeded in limiting or reducing youth exposure to alcohol advertising on television. In congressional hearings in 2003, Beer Institute president Jeff Becker referred to the standard as "proportional" because approximately 30 percent of the population is under age 21.

Of the population under 21, children under age two are not counted for television ratings by Nielsen. Of two- to 20-year-olds' exposure to alcohol product advertising between 2001 and 2007, 68 percent fell on 12- to 20-year-olds, a group that Nielsen reports only made up 47 percent of the two to 20 age group. Federal surveys begin measuring underage drinking at age 12, and the small amount of drinking among 12-year-olds suggests that 12- to 20-year-olds are the group at greatest risk of underage drinking. The U.S. Census Bureau estimates that this group is 13 percent of the population.

Recognizing that 30 percent is not a proportional standard when viewed in the light of the population at greatest risk, the

National Research Council and Institute of Medicine, as well as 20 state attorneys general, have called on the industry to consider changing its standard to eliminate advertising on programming with more than 15 percent youth (ages 12–20) in its audiences. A 15 percent standard would reduce overall youth exposure to alcohol advertisements by 20 percent, according to CAMY research estimates, saving lives and even saving the industry some money in advertising costs.

"Or is it because those already disposed to drinking are more attuned to alcohol advertising?"

Alcohol Advertising Does Not Target Children

Trevor Butterworth and Rebecca Goldin, PhD

In the following viewpoint, Trevor Butterworth and Rebecca Goldin, PhD, make counter-allegations that alcohol brands deliberately target minors in magazines. The authors maintain that ad placements are based on cost and circulation, not the percentage of young readers. Butterworth and Goldin uphold that publications that expose children and adolescents to such advertisements are aimed at primarily adult readers. Youth and alcohol advertising is a concern, but its link to underage drinking is a controversial and separate issue, the authors argue. Butterworth is a senior fellow and editor at STATS (Statistical Assessment Service), a nonprofit organization that focuses on statistics in the media, where Goldin is director of research.

Trevor Butterworth and Rebecca Goldin, PhD, "Targeting Youth? Alcohol Advertising in Magazines," *STATS*, August 1, 2006. www.stats.org. Reproduced by permission.

As you read, consider the following questions:

1. Why is the Center on Alcohol Marketing and Youth's measurement of alcohol advertisements in magazines problematic, as stated by Trevor Butterworth and Rebecca Goldin, PhD?

2. What data do the authors provide to base their claim that underage drinking is in decline?

3. If alcohol ads influence bad behavior, what do the authors recommend?

D o alcohol manufacturers target advertising at youth? This question has plagued parents, advocacy groups, social researchers and even the government for years. Organizations such as the Center for Alcohol Marketing and Youth (CAMY) have steadfastly claimed that they do, and that these ads contribute to the problem of underage drinking. In April 2005, after tabulating the number and type of ads found in magazines and other media, CAMY analyzed the data and appeared to come up with a definitive empirically-grounded answer: As the *New York Times* reported,

> "56 percent of spending on beer and liquor ads that ran from 2001 through 2003 appeared in publications with a disproportionate readership among those ages 12 to 20."

CAMY's research was and is widely cited, for example the *Boston Globe* reported in August 2005 that

> "girls are specific targets of Marketing . . . [and] get a heavier exposure to alcohol marketing than girls of legal age, and see 95 percent more alcohol advertising than the typical 35-year-old. Much of it is in the magazines girls read, especially, *Cosmopolitan, In Style, Vibe, Entertainment Weekly* and *Vogue*."

Or as the *Oregonian* reported in November of the same year [2005],

The Scientific Conclusion

Alcohol ads neither increase drinking nor cause non-drinkers to become drinkers. That's the conclusion of scientific research conducted for decades around the world by governments, health agencies, and universities. Successful alcohol ads can increase a producer's share of the market, which it obtains at the expense of its competitors' share.

David J. Hanson,
"Explosion of Alcohol Ads on Cable Television."
www2.potsdam.edu/hansondj.

"Alcohol is the No. 1 drug problem among teenagers, says researcher David Jernigan, who runs the Washington, D.C.-based Center on Alcohol Marketing and Youth [CAMY]."

"'It is so critical that parents be aware of what our kids are facing and speak up about it,' he says, 'because what the advertising industry says is: It's all the parents' responsibility.'"

But in the July [2006] issue of *Contemporary Economic Policy*, Jon Nelson, professor emeritus of economics at Penn State, challenged the conventional wisdom with research that found that alcohol advertisers did not, in fact, target youth. According to Nelson, the most influential factors for where ads are placed in magazines are cost and size of circulation and not the percentage of young readers.

Apart from a United Press International [UPI] wire story, no media organization reported the study in the United States, despite deep concern about underage drinking, its causes and remedies. Are the media at fault for ignoring this study? The question can only be answered by comparing CAMY's approach with Nelson's.

Targeting—So Who's Right?

In part, the answer to whether the alcohol industry targets teens depends on what you mean by "targeting." According to CAMY, targeting occurs whenever alcohol companies advertise in magazines with a youth readership over 15 percent— "youth" in this case being defined as being between the ages of 12 and 20 (for some reason CAMY doesn't think 11-year-olds read popular magazines). The percentage of youth in this age group in the population is about 14 percent, so, CAMY reasons, a magazine that appeals to more youth than the population average is one that alcohol companies *would avoid* if they weren't "targeting" youth.

Magazines that fall into this category include *Sports Illustrated*, *Popular Mechanics*, *Rolling Stone*, *Vogue*, and others. From a statistical point of view, these magazines "oversample" youth, meaning that they have a disproportionately high youth readership compared to the general population. For CAMY, any advertisement for alcohol in such a magazine is automatically targeting youth.

CAMY's argument is bolstered by a *per capita* exposure rate: Underage youth see more adds for beer, wine, distilled spirits, and alcopops than those over age 21 (though the amount of additional exposure is decreasing).

But this measurement is controversial: While most of us are worried about very young kids becoming turned on to alcohol, the per capita exposure rates mixes in young adults between the ages of 18 to 20. For the alcohol companies, these underage drinkers are difficult to avoid when "intentionally" targeting people age 21 and over. And these are not typically the kind of "young" people whose parents are rallying behind cries to limit alcohol advertising.

Implicit in CAMY's language is that alcohol companies are purposefully looking for youth in order to advertise to them. But CAMY neglects to mention that alcohol companies do not advertise in magazines whose main audience is youth; for example, *Seventeen* and *YM* do not accept alcohol ads. Magazines that target youth are generally alcohol-ad free.

Furthermore, the magazines that CAMY refers to are not primarily written for (or sold to) underage youth. In most cases, more than 80 percent of their readership is of legal drinking age. So is "targeting" a fair word for alcohol advertisements in these magazines? Are the alcohol companies really after underage drinkers?

Penn State's study evaluates whether companies are actually *motivated* by higher rates of young readers. Nelson identifies several factors that might affect an advertising decision—the size of the readership, the cost of the advertisement, the percentage of youth readers, sales outlets, demographics such as race and income, and magazine topic. The question is which factor actually influences how companies make marketing decisions?

According to Nelson's research, the proportion of young readers among the readership did not make much difference. The influential factors were the size of the audience (not just how many people bought the magazine, but how many actually read it), and how much an ad costs per 1,000 copies in circulation.

Unlike CAMY's method which *defines* targeting to be an adolescent readership over 15 percent, Nelson's work suggests economic models for how alcohol companies make their marketing decisions, with a testable hypothesis as to whether marketing decisions are influenced by larger proportions of adolescent readers. In none of the models was adolescent readership an influential factor.

This study suggests that we should move away from accusing the advertising industry of plotting to get kids involved with alcohol before they're 21. However, if we view it not as a matter of evil-alcohol-company intent, but as a moral issue, we can't just dismiss the fact that kids are indeed exposed to alcohol advertising through magazine ads, and more than adults.

One Side of the Story

Whether this exposure affects how much those under 21 drink is an entirely different, and much more controversial, question. Some studies find that kids who report drinking more also report seeing more ads; but is it because the advertising *causes* them to drink—or is it because those already disposed to drinking are more attuned to alcohol advertising? Culture is also a powerful influence: Something legal and popular with adults (for millennia) is going to be perceived in a positive way by teenagers; the desire to appear grown up and sophisticated, and to enjoy the good life is not something that was created by advertising or alcohol companies, it is imbibed from real life.

At the same time, research data shows that kids are drinking less. According to [the study] Monitoring the Future, *"The longer-term trend data available for 12th graders show that alcohol usage rates, and binge drinking in particular, are substantially below where they were at the beginning of the 1980s."* After an uptick in the first half of the 1990s, the downward trend has resumed.

But here's a thought: If we could prove that ads unduly influence behavior of adolescents, why not propose a ban on alcohol advertising entirely (as does the American Medical Association [AMA])? Or why not legislate that magazines such as *Sports Illustrated* and *Vogue* should only be sold to people over 21? Of course, that might raise some eyebrows, considering pornographic magazines are available to those aged 18.

Either way, we cannot have an informed, rational, and productive conversation about underage drinking if the media only cover one side of the story. It's a cliché in this kind of discussion to use the word "sober" in some wry way; but without sober evaluation of the social science data by reporters, how are we ever going to arrive at public policies that will actually work?

Periodical Bibliography

The following articles have been selected to supplement the diverse views presented in this chapter.

Lillian Daniel	"Kid Stuff: Raising Children in a Consumer Culture," *Christian Century*, January 11, 2005.
Jason Eberhart-Phillips	"Alcohol Advertising Feeds Kids a Big Lie," *Sacramento Bee*, May 3, 2007.
Sarah Ebner	"Is the Princess Stereotype Harming Our Daughters?" *Times Online* (United Kingdom), August 4, 2009. www.timesonline.co.uk.
Allen D. Kanner	"Today's Class Brought to You By. . ." *Tikkun*, January/February 2008.
Douglas MacMillan	"Alcohol, Then Tobacco. Now Fast Food?" *BusinessWeek*, June 30, 2009.
Kathleen McGrory	"Dade Schools Eye Advertising Revenue," *Miami Herald*, February 11, 2008.
Neil Merrett	"Kids of All Ages Targeted Next in Soft Drink Shift," BeverageDaily.com, December 4, 2008. www.beveragedaily.com.
Nicola Pinson	"Soda Contracts: Who Really Benefits?" *Rethinking Schools Online*, Summer 2006. www.rethinkingschools.org.
Tom Scocca	"Can You Tell Me How to Get Diapers Without Sesame Street Characters on Them?" *Slate*, September 30, 2009.
Harry A. Valetk	"Child-Proofing Your Ads: New Maine Law Restricts Marketing to Minors," Law.com, August 4, 2009. www.law.com.

OPPOSING
VIEWPOINTS®
SERIES

CHAPTER 3

Should Political Advertising Be Reformed?

Chapter Preface

In July 2008, presidential candidate John McCain attacked the popularity of his rival, Barack Obama, with a television ad. Calling him "the biggest celebrity in the world," the thirty-second spot compared Obama to pop star Britney Spears and socialite Paris Hilton and challenged his preparedness for the White House. "But is he ready to lead?" the commercial asked. "With gas prices soaring, Barack Obama says no to offshore drilling. And he says he'll raise taxes on electricity. Higher taxes, more foreign oil, that's the real Obama."

McCain's political ad got noticed. Hilton entered the ring with a parody in which she presented her "energy policy for America." Obama's spokesman, Tommy Vietor, responded with a statement that alluded to a hit song by Spears: "On a day when major news organizations across the country are taking Senator McCain to task for a steady stream of false, negative attacks, his campaign has launched yet another. Or, as some might say, 'Oops! He did it again.'"[1]

Both McCain and Obama had aired a record-breaking one hundred thousand political ads by that stage, according to the Wisconsin Advertising Project (WiscAds) at the University of Wisconsin. The numbers were up 30 percent compared to George W. Bush and John Kerry during the 2004 elections. The Wisconsin Advertising Project also stated that by October 2008, 73 percent of McCain's and 61 percent of Obama's ads had made a sharp turn toward the negative. Another analysis by communications professor William Benoit reported that the attack ad blitz reached a high point in 2008. "The only campaign in history that matches this level of negativity was in the first ever presidential TV spot campaign when Dwight Eisenhower had negative attacks in 69 percent of his ad statements,"[2] he said. The authors in the following chapter investigate the effectiveness and issues of political advertising.

Notes

1. *Boston Globe*, July 30, 2008. www.boston.com.
2. *ScienceDaily*, November 1, 2008. www.sciencedaily.com.

| "*[2008's] presidential election ads could be the most negative since the dawn of the television era.*"

Political Advertising Is Becoming Increasingly Negative

June Kronholz

In the following viewpoint, June Kronholz argues that political advertisements during the 2008 elections were harsher than ever. She charges, however, that they were also more misleading and unsuccessful. For example, presidential candidate John McCain's commercial connecting his rival, Barack Obama, to a former radical did not resonate with timely concerns, Kronholz says. She does concede that attack ads focus on important issues and are more likely to be factually supported. But negative campaigns create more negativity, the author upholds, and exposed inaccuracies and errors in political ads are drowned out by partisan rhetoric. Kronholz is a staff reporter for the Wall Street Journal.

June Kronholz, "Ready, Aim, Backfire: Nasty Political Ads Fall Flat," *Wall Street Journal*, October 16, 2008. Republished with permission of Wall Street Journal, conveyed through Copyright Clearance Center, Inc.

As you read, consider the following questions:

1. What historical examples of negative political ads does June Kronholz provide?

2. According to the author, why do political scientists support attack ads?

3. What does Darrell West say about deception in negative political ads?

This year's [2008's] presidential election ads could be the most negative since the dawn of the television era, political scientists say. There are more of them, and they are more wantonly misleading.

They may also be the least successful ever.

Sens. John McCain and Barack Obama have both engaged in personal attacks in recent weeks. Sen. McCain's current ads attempt to link Sen. Obama to 1960s Chicago radical William Ayers to back up the McCain campaign's contention that the Democrat is "too risky for America." Sen. Obama's return-fire spots tied Sen. McCain to a 1980s savings and loan scandal because of his help in the Senate for one of the executives.

But polls suggest that Sen. McCain isn't only running more negative advertising, he is losing more ground for it.

The rules haven't changed, political scientists say. A deft negative ad, like Sen. McCain's spot questioning the substance behind Sen. Obama's extraordinary celebrity, still can send an opponent reeling.

The roiling economy means that times have. "You can't create a concern that doesn't already exist," says Brookings Institution scholar Darrell West.

Rule No. 1 of negative campaigning is that it must be about an issue that already worries voters. President Lyndon Johnson's infamous 1964 Daisy ad, which implied that Republican opponent Barry Goldwater would use the atom bomb, played to voters' concerns about a nuclear war. George H.W.

Bush's 1988 Willie Horton ad against Democratic challenger Michael Dukakis tapped voters' fears about rising crime rates.

But aging radicals and old scandals don't tap today's fears, which may be why they haven't resonated. "Arguing about personal associations pales in comparison" to the current grim economic news, says Dr. West.

Independent studies say a higher proportion of Sen. McCain's ads are negative than Sen. Obama's. And with voters largely blaming Republicans for the economy, polls suggest that Sen. McCain is paying the price for the increasingly negative tone of the campaign. In the past, voters usually divided the blame for negative advertising between both candidates, says Dr. West. Among recent elections, "there's none that come close" to today's one-sided leveling of blame, he adds.

In a stark indication of how that tone is affecting the campaign, the Arizona senator was forced to urge his supporters to be "respectful" of Sen. Obama after the Democratic candidate was jeered at some recent McCain rallies.

In an Ipsos public affairs poll released Wednesday [October 15, 2008], 53% of voters said Sen. McCain engaged in more negative campaigning than Sen. Obama did, while 30% said it was Sen. Obama who was more negative. The disparity was even greater—61% to 31%—in a New York Times/CBS News poll also released Wednesday.

In the Ipsos poll, 57% of voters said the ads aren't effective.

New Outlets

Negative campaigning has been around as long as there have been campaigns, of course. Abraham Lincoln's opponents whispered he was the son of a slave woman. Federalists warned that incest would be taught in the schools if Thomas Jefferson were elected. In 1948, with World War II just ended, Harry Truman compared Republicans to [Adolf] Hitler.

Running a Positive and a Negative Track

There's another reason campaigns are so quick to employ, and often abuse, negative ads. Unlike Bud Light, which seeks to maximize its public appeal, political campaigns can afford to alienate the more sensitive members of the electorate and are perfectly happy to drive down turnout—as long as they win votes from a plurality of those who do show up. In fact, one reason campaigns bother running positive ads when a race turns nasty is to ensure that their negative ads remain effective. This is known in the trade as "running a positive and a negative track." Craig Varoga, a Democratic consultant, says, "If people feel somewhat good about you, they're more likely to believe the accusations you make against the other side." No surprise, then, that campaigns are willing to go for blood.

Joshua Green, "Dumb and Dumber,"
Atlantic, July-August 2004.

Candidates have found new outlets for their ads since then—television and the Internet instead of newspapers and broadsides—and the number of ads has soared. Sen. McCain aired TV ads 5,510 times in 10 key media markets during a Sept. 28–Oct. 4 [2008] survey week, reports the Wisconsin Advertising Project, which is run by the University of Wisconsin's political science department.

Sen. Obama aired his ads 8,961 times in many of the same markets, and together the presidential candidates spent $28 million on TV time that week. That's $10 million more than president George W. Bush and his Democratic challenger, John Kerry, spent in a similar week in 2004.

Even though voters say they don't like them, negative ads may not be a bad thing, political scientists say. Attack ads are more likely to be about issues than are positive ads. They're likely to contain more information, back up their claims with evidence and delve into details.

Of 14 largely negative ads that Mr. Bush and Al Gore ran against each other in 2000, 13 backed up their claims with some proof, says Vanderbilt University political scientist John Geer, who has examined 795 presidential campaign ads that aired between 1960 and 2000. Of 19 positive ads from the same campaign, only one offered any evidence.

The stronger the attack, the more verification it usually contains, Dr. Geer adds. Sen. McCain's ad about Mr. Ayers, the 1960s radical, includes 13 citations, mostly newspaper reports. Sen. Obama's savings and loan ad uses newsreel footage of a Senate committee's rebuke of Sen. McCain.

All that creates a national vetting process: A damaged candidate will be revealed, while a capable candidate will more easily assure the public he or she is ready for the Oval Office.

Economic fears account for some of this year's largely unrestrained negativity. Voters who overwhelmingly tell pollsters that the country is "on the wrong track" are more likely to believe a negative ad than an uplifting message like president Ronald Reagan's 1984 "Morning in America" spot.

Other Causes

But there are other causes for the negative tone. Voters perceive that the stakes are especially high this year, inciting more partisanship and emboldening candidates to make sharper attacks. That's easy when the candidates have distinctly different views about the Iraq war, taxation and medical insurance.

Negativity unchecked tends to amount to more negativity. Ad-watch columns in newspapers shamed campaigns for using inaccurate information when these features first appeared in 1988, but have lost much of their watchdog effectiveness this year, political scientists say. Their reviews, which generally run only once, are overwhelmed by an ad that may air thousands of times. With broadcast outlets and the Internet increasingly partisan, voters also can dismiss a negative review of their candidate's ads as media bias. "There's no penalty for deception. If anything, there are short-term rewards," says Dr. West of Brookings.

Campaigns also increasingly air provocative ads in an effort to generate free media coverage. Sen. McCain ran an ad alleging that Sen. Obama voted for sex education for kindergartners while he was in the Illinois Senate. Sen. Obama in fact had voted for a broad bill that would, among other things, teach kindergartners about sexual predators.

The kindergartner ad was widely derided and ran only briefly. But it prompted hundreds of news stories that repeated Sen. McCain's charge and sent reporters for a fresh review of Sen. Obama's legislative record.

The increasingly negative tone of the campaign isn't likely to be lost on voters, particularly those in the swing-state media markets where the candidates are concentrating their attention. During the Wisconsin project's survey week in late September [2008], the campaigns ran ads 1,991 times in Denver—about 12 ads an hour—and 1,300 times in Las Vegas.

Almost all of the McCain ads and one-third of the Obama ads were negative.

For Sen. McCain, those ads are an attempt to find a new message, change the national conversation and turn around the campaign. Dr. Geer, who has written a book titled *In Defense of Negativity: Attack Ads in Presidential Campaigns*, insists that's the price of democracy.

"You have to say what's wrong with the status quo in order to change it," he says.

"It's time to stand up in defense of the much-maligned attack ad."

Negative Political Advertising Is Necessary

David Mark

David Mark is senior editor of Politico, *an online political magazine, and author of* Going Dirty: The Art of Negative Campaigning. *In the following viewpoint, Mark insists that negative political advertising plays an important role in elections. In a media-intensive era, he states that attack ads can be counteracted immediately, creating exchanges that provide a wealth of information about the candidates. Also, the author maintains that they are better documented and more specific than positive ads. In fact, candidates must go negative to reveal their opponents' shortcomings and demonstrate how their stances on policies and issues differ, observes Mark.*

As you read, consider the following questions:

1. How, according to David Mark, has the Information Age changed responses to negative ads?

David Mark, "Attack Ads Are Good for You!" *Reason*, November 2006. Copyright © 2006 by Reason Foundation, 3415 S. Sepulveda Blvd., Suite 400, Los Angeles, CA 90034, www.reason.com. Reproduced by permission.

2. How does the author explain voter distaste for attack ads?

3. How does the author describe positive ads?

Michael Steele encountered tough financial times in the late 1990s. Though he earned a law degree at Georgetown in 1991, the Maryland Republican failed the bar exams in his home state and in Washington, D.C. As a result, his practice at a large international law firm in Washington was limited in the high-end work it could perform and in the fees it could charge.

Steele eventually struck out on his own, founding the Steele Group, a business and legal consulting firm in suburban Prince George's County, Maryland. It seems the business rarely made a profit; Steele says it encountered financial challenges when clients didn't pay their bills. The firm eventually dissolved, and Steele's personal debts mounted. By 2002, according to financial disclosure reports, he had borrowed $35,000 through a line of credit against his home.

A fuller picture of Steele's money situation at that time remains clouded, due to gaps in his résumé and his unwillingness to detail past finances. What is clear is that while his finances were plummeting, his political star was on the rise. He moved up quickly from local party activist to state Republican Party chairman and, in 2003, to lieutenant governor of Maryland, becoming the first black person of either party elected to statewide office.

Steele is now a candidate for the U.S. Senate. When Democrats raise questions about his past personal money woes, he dismisses them as negative campaigning, suggesting his opaque financial past has no bearing on public policy decisions. "What does it matter to any voter whether or not you paid a bill on time?" Steele asked in a September 2005 radio interview, shortly before declaring his Senate candidacy. "There has to be, I think, a veil of privacy, even around public figures. The expectation is, to run for office doesn't mean I turn over everything I've ever done in my life for you to sit in judgment of. It's one of the reasons why it is very difficult to find individuals who are capable, competent, and committed to public service who want to get into this business."

Steele is hardly alone in his professed outrage at aggressive campaign tactics. Politicians routinely try to shift attention away from issues of public concern, playing the victim of unfair, invasive attacks. But is closely examining a candidate's questionable financial history wrong? Senators, after all, spend hundreds of billions of taxpayer dollars. Shouldn't potentially germane information about Steele's financial history be available to voters, who can decide for themselves whether it is relevant to his qualifications?

Negative campaigning is an issue across the country this fall [2006], in campaigns from Massachusetts to Hawaii and in races down the ballot from U.S. senator to county assessor. As wounded politicians whine that such speech is out of bounds, it's time to stand up in defense of the much-maligned attack ad. In this age of instantaneous information via blogs, round-the-clock cable coverage, and other media, political attacks can be swiftly countered. Any opinion offered about a candidate, no matter how mean, vile, or sinister, can be rebutted immediately and globally. Thanks to such exchanges, voters this year will know a lot about prospective elected officials if they are willing to process multiple sources of information and draw their own conclusions.

Voters Hate Negativity—Except When They Like It

Many people recoil at negative political ads. Indeed, *negative campaigning* has become a catch-all phrase that implies there is something inherently wrong with criticizing an opponent. It is one of the most bemoaned aspects of the American political system, particularly by academics and journalists who say it lowers the level of discourse and intensifies divisions among voters.

The dim academic view of negative campaigning was reflected in an influential 1999 *Political Science Review* study by Arizona State University political scientists Patrick J. Kenney and Kim Fridkin, titled *Do Negative Campaigns Mobilize or Suppress Turnout? Clarifying the Relationship Between Negativity and Participation.* "Our most troubling finding is that negative or attack advertising actually suppresses turnout," Kenney and Fridkin wrote. "We would even go so far as to say that negative advertisements may pose a serious antidemocratic threat."

Journalists often reach similar conclusions. Take the 2006 California Democratic gubernatorial primary, during which the tactics of candidates Phil Angelides, the state treasurer, and Steve Westly, the state controller, prompted intense criticism. Each sought the right to face off against Republican Gov. Arnold Schwarzenegger, and the campaign run-up to the June primary quickly devolved into a series of harsh verbal exchanges about the candidates' environmental records, proclivity to raise taxes, and other issues. Angelides won the primary but earned the ire of editorialists for going negative. Among the critics was Martin F. Nolan, a former reporter and editor for the *Boston Globe*, who wrote in a *San Francisco Chronicle* op-ed piece shortly after the race, "Negative campaigning reduces turnout and alienates occasional voters who would otherwise consider voting for a fresh face."

This conventional wisdom is dead wrong, argues the Vanderbilt political scientist John Geer, author of the 2006 book *In Defense of Negativity: Attack Ads in Presidential Campaigns.* "Journalists and academics think of negative campaigning as personal attacks," says Geer. "I don't particularly worry about it. It's going to take something a little more consequential to hurt this country than some rough 30-second spots."

Geer's research demonstrates that negative ads tend to be more substantive than positive spots, because to be credible they must be better documented and specific. His analysis of television campaign advertising from 1960 through 2004 found that nearly three-quarters of the claims in negative spots involved issues, not attacks on candidates' characters or values. "You can't just attack [former] President [George W.] Bush for being weak on the economy," Geer says. "You need to be more specific when you attack. You have to say why. For the attacks to work, they have to be based on fact."

There is considerable reason to believe the electorate appreciates negative campaigning. While studies like Kenney and Fridkin's suggest the practice can turn voters off, voting participation statistics demonstrate that the toughest, most partisan races often bring more people to the polls. The 2004 presidential campaign was one of the most heated in recent memory, punctuated by thrusts and parries over Sen. John Kerry's Vietnam service, charges of deadly policy failures in Iraq, and warnings that electing the opposition could lead to further terrorist attacks. That same campaign produced a voter turnout of roughly 60 percent, the highest in 36 years. Kerry's vote total was up 16 percent from vice president Al Gore's in 2000; president George W. Bush's vote total was 23 percent higher than it had been four years before.

Those numbers fit a historical pattern. Turnout rose during the years following the Civil War, when campaigns were very biting. This was a period when Republicans were accused of "waving the bloody shirt" from the military conflict of recent memory and Democrats were labeled "disloyal" for supporting the Confederacy, or at least being lukewarm on maintaining the Union.

Or consider the infamous 1984 grudge match of a Senate race in North Carolina, where incumbent Republican Jesse Helms faced a stiff challenge from moderate Democratic Gov. Jim Hunt. The candidates raised large sums of money to pay for a full menu of negative campaign tactics: personal attacks, below-the-radar smears by allies, a series of combative de-

The Fine Tradition of Negativity

The fine tradition of negativity and attacks goes back to the nation's founding document. By the count of political scientist John G. Geer of Vanderbilt University, 70 percent of the statements in the Declaration of Independence are not uplifting promises of more-just and democratic governance, but attacks on England and George III ("He has obstructed the Administration of Justice," "He has dissolved Representative Houses" and, of course, "He has plundered our seas, ravaged our coasts, burnt our towns, and destroyed the lives of our people"). These criticisms "provided the basis for thinking about abuses of power and the centrality of certain basic human rights," Geer writes in his 2006 book *In Defense of Negativity: Attack Ads in Presidential Campaigns.* "Without such negativity, the argument for establishing a new nation that 'derived its just powers from the consent of the govern[ed]' would not have been possible."

Sharon Begley,
"Ready, Aim, Fire!" Newsweek,
vol. 152, no. 16, October 20, 2008.

bates. For that vitriolic campaign 68 percent of registered voters turned out at the polls. A more modest 60 percent cast ballots in the state's 2004 senatorial race, which coincided with the heated presidential battle. The state's prior Senate race, an open seat contest during the 2002 midterm elections, brought out a measly 40 percent of registered Tar Heel voters.

As Michael Barone, coauthor of the *Almanac of American Politics*, noted shortly after the 2004 election, "Enthusiasm in politics usually contains a large element of hatred."

Ugly Truth Tellers

Few if any officeholders will openly admit to negative campaigning. To candidates, criticizing an opponent's voting record is properly called *comparative advertising*, and spotlighting a rival's marital infidelity is merely *raising character issues*. Campaign tactics that to one voter seem misleading, mean-spirited, or immoral can impart to another important and relevant information about how the candidate would perform under the pressures of public office. Negative campaigning, like beauty, is in the eye of the beholder.

Voter distaste for negative campaigning is understandable, if only because the form and content of political ads are so different from what people usually see in commercial spots. Anyone peddling breakfast cereal needs to be careful about criticizing competitors too overtly or else run the risk of turning off consumers. Rarely do product advertisements include direct comparisons to rival products, and when they occur the contrasts are usually mild and fleeting. As a result, viewers are often shocked at the stark criticisms offered in political ads, particularly when they're sandwiched between softer spots. . . .

Each race has its own local nuances, but some negative campaign themes are pervasive. Republicans contend their opponents are soft on terror and itching to raise taxes. Democrats portray Republicans as surrogates for president George W. Bush, trying to weigh them down with the burden of his low approval ratings; they cite the Iraq situation, high gas prices, stagnant wages, and scores of other issues. Republicans often try to neutralize such criticism by accusing the Democrats of "pessimism"—a charge heatedly denied by members of the minority party, who describe themselves as tellers of difficult truths.

The pessimism taunt is a time-honored way to duck fair questions, says William G. Mayer, a political scientist at Northeastern University. "This year, you will see a lot of Democratic ads talking about the failures of the Bush administration," he explains. "Some of those make quite valid points." Even in cases where charges contain only a kernel of truth, he argues, they raise important issues voters otherwise might not have considered. Positive ads, featuring happy family pictures and lists of accomplishments, do not provide enough information for voters to make informed decisions. What a candidate chooses not to discuss is usually as important as what he or she prefers to emphasize.

"No candidate is likely to provide a full and frank discussion of his own shortcomings," Mayer wrote in his seminal 1996 *Political Science Quarterly* article "In Defense of Negative Campaigning." "Such issues will only get a proper hearing if an opponent is allowed to talk about them by engaging in negative campaigning." Challengers in particular must go negative to demonstrate the flaws in the policies supported by the incumbent and show how they would do things differently.

Credit Crunch in Maryland

Although Michael Steele is not running as an incumbent, it's not surprising that Maryland Democrats would push hard to find information that reflected poorly on him as his Senate bid ramped up. Tall, suave, and debonair, Steele poses a potentially serious challenge to their party's hold on black voters, a crucial element of Democratic support whose defection would make it nearly impossible to win statewide elections.

Steele often shares his inspiring up-by-the-bootstraps personal story. Born at Andrews Air Force Base in Prince George's County, he was raised in a working-class family in Washington, D.C. His mother was a laundress who refused to go on welfare because she did not want the government raising her children.

Steele has said Ronald Reagan's 1976 insurgent candidacy for the GOP's presidential nomination led him to become a Republican. He spent three years in a Jesuit seminary after graduating from Johns Hopkins, then switched to a legal career. With his emphasis on entrepreneurship and his solidly conservative views on social issues, he quickly caught the notice of Republican higher-ups. In 1995 the state GOP selected him as Maryland State Republican Man of the Year. He worked on several political campaigns and served as an alternate delegate to the 1996 Republican National Convention in San Diego and as a delegate to the 2000 Republican National Convention in Philadelphia.

In December 2000 Steele was elected chairman of the Maryland Republican Party, becoming the first African American ever to lead a state GOP. Republican gubernatorial nominee Robert Ehrlich selected Steele as his running mate in 2002. They won, becoming the first Republican ticket in 36 years to occupy the state's top elected jobs.

But the campaign was often bruising. During that race Steele faced repeated questions about his financial past. He admitted that sometime during his career he had faced financial difficulties. But he was vague, and his biographies do not account for all the years between his college graduation, his time in seminary, his marriage, his law school graduation, the founding of his own business, and his time in office.

Questions about Steele's financial history became increasingly acute in fall 2002, when the Maryland Republican Party began paying him $5,000 a month in consulting fees shortly after his selection as Ehrlich's running mate. Democrats said the payments raised ethical questions, charging that the Republicans had essentially hired a candidate. State Republican Party officials defended the payments by saying Steele was being paid to continue performing his duties as party chairman because his replacement was not prepared to take over yet.

Similar questions were sure to emerge again during his Senate bid, which Steele made official in fall 2005, a few months after Democratic Sen. Paul Sarbanes announced he would retire. But Steele caught a lucky break through

Democrats' clumsy attempts to dig up damaging information. In July 2005 Lauren B. Weiner, a researcher working for the Democratic Senatorial Campaign Committee (DSCC), illegally obtained a copy of Steele's credit report. The *Washington Post* reported that "sources familiar with the episode said Steele's credit report was obtained with the use of his Social Security number, which was found on a public court document." Weiner used Steele's Social Security number to obtain his credit report from TransUnion and used DSCC research director Katie Barge's DSCC credit card to pay for the report. Weiner pleaded guilty to a misdemeanor charge of computer fraud and agreed to complete 150 hours of community service. Barge resigned.

Steele then went on the offensive, saying public figures deserve some privacy. He publicly warned fellow Republican Senate candidates around the country to beware of credit hackers and threatened a civil suit against the former Democratic operatives. The Democrats' ham-handedness has largely diffused outstanding questions about Steele's finances.

That's unfortunate. Obtaining a credit report under fraudulent auspices is wrong. But voters deserve to have the fullest possible accounting of candidates' financial backgrounds, which can shed light on their financial judgment. Steele was able to play the victim while deflecting important questions related to how he might spend taxpayer dollars.

All of this is not to say that Steele's past business woes and problems paying bills render him unqualified to serve in the Senate. Such a standard would sideline many intelligent, hard-working, well-intentioned people who have weathered money problems. But voters have the right to decide such information's relevance for themselves. . . .

> *"Clearly, providing free airtime doesn't
> limit speech, it expands it."*

Candidates Should Be Given Free Airtime

Marj Halperin

*In the following viewpoint, Marj Halperin advocates the allot-
ment of free television airtime to political candidates during
elections. She argues that underfunded, worthy challengers unable to purchase costly television advertisements are not considered viable, with the current system tilting toward deep-pocketed
incumbents. Contrary to the assertions of major broadcasters
and conservatives, Halperin states that free airtime protects, not
threatens, free speech and would ensure that each candidate is
given a chance to be equally heard. The author is a communications consultant and campaign strategist based in Chicago, Illinois.*

As you read, consider the following questions:

1. According to Marj Halperin, how would John McCain
   have been more successful at his efforts for campaign
   finance reform?

Marj Halperin, "Show Me the Air Time," *American Prospect*, April 16, 2007. Reproduced
with permission from The American Prospect, 11 Beacon Street, Suite 1120, Boston,
MA 02108.

2. How does Halperin support her allegation that candidates that spend the most on their campaigns are favored to win elections?

3. What did the Our Democracy, Our Airwaves Act set to accomplish, as stated by the author?

When [late-night TV show host] David Letterman hosted [presidential candidate] Barack Obama last week [April 2007], he broke out of his comedy mode for a moment of serious commentary. After heralding Obama's announcement that he'd raked in some $25 million in the crucial first-quarter fund-raising period, Letterman gently prodded, "Why is this so essential for such high-profile candidates to have this kind of early money?"

Obama gave a dodgy reply coated in humor: "We've got to advertise on the Letterman show. Most of the money goes into television." But he added a pitch for real campaign finance reform, saying, "I think it would be preferable if we had some form of public financing or free television time, but I think your bosses at CBS wouldn't go for that." A chastened Letterman whispered agreement, then abruptly changed the subject to the brouhaha over David Geffen's spat with the Clintons.

Candidates Without Money Are Not Viable

Indeed, the tens of millions already raised by would-be presidential nominees indicate that the 2008 election cycle will no doubt be a highly profitable one for Letterman's bosses and other TV executives. Candidates who don't raise enough money to get their message on TV—and consistently repeat it—aren't considered viable. And it takes increasingly more money to buy the airtime to disseminate that message; hence, the increasingly high stakes for this early primary fund-raising period. To get an idea of how fast this fund-raising threshold has risen, consider that the prior record for this period was held by Al Gore, who raised "only" $8.9 million in 1999's first quarter.

For roughly 48 hours, it looked like Hillary Clinton had won the early fund-raising sweepstakes with $26 million, around $19 million of which can be spent on the primary race. Technically, she still holds the top spot, but Obama took the fun—and the meaning—out of her win. He held back and dropped his $25.7 million total like a bomb at the end of the news cycle, giving him a tactical victory in this critical fund-raising period ending March 31 [2007].

The Clinton camp is on the defensive. Obama's figure is made all the more powerful by both his lower expectations and by the fact that he raised his money "mostly from small donors," as he likes to brag. Obama told Letterman, "90 percent of the folks who donated on the Web site barackobama .com gave $100 or less." This will enable Obama to spend $24.8 million of his money in the primary. As anyone who donated to his campaign will know, that's because his team was ruthless in its push to amass as many individual donors as possible at—but not above—the $2,300 per person limit for primary contributions. Those who gave less are good targets for appeals to give again.

As the story continues to unfold, we're seeing that some candidates have already spent significant portions of their first-quarter money. But Clinton, who was fortunate to start with a bigger cache than Obama, ends the period with the most primary funds on hand.

There are several ways to slice and dice this information, but the result is generally the same: The candidate with a terrific message but little money to buy TV spots is like the tree in the woods. Nobody hears him (or her) fall. And Democratic trailer John Edwards, with his paltry $14 million, is likely turning to petrified wood.

Compared to the Democratic contenders, the GOP [Grand Old Party] hopefuls aren't exactly having a record-breaking year. Raising $20.7 million secured a surprise lead for Mitt Romney (who, no doubt, wishes he could show that kind of strength in public opinion polls). He tried to boost that number by $2.35 million with a personal loan, which isn't included in his total. Even without the self-donation, Romney easily holds the lead over second-ranked Rudy Giuliani, who reported just $14.7 million. And an embarrassing $13 million fund-raising total forced John McCain to delay his official declaration of candidacy in favor of a campaign overhaul.

Fighting the Symptom

It's ironic that McCain, a champion of campaign finance reform, is the Republican most at risk of falling after this first-quarter fund-raising report. David King, a professor at Harvard University's John F. Kennedy School of Government, quipped to CNN, "For McCain, it looks like he's made campaign finance reform work. Everyone knew he didn't like the role of money in politics, but one would have hoped he would have liked the role of money in his own campaign. He's now coming to this race a day late and $12 million short."

When the McCain-sponsored Bipartisan Campaign Reform Act was enacted in 2002, his biggest victory was the legislation's soft-money ban. But the continued prominence of PACs [political action committees] and groups such as Swift Boat Veterans for Truth [now known as Swift Vets and POWs for Truth] has proven campaign finance to be the uncontrollable hydra [mythical multiheaded serpent] of American politics. Cut off one head and it grows two more. For all his efforts, McCain has made little headway in improving the increasingly obscene presidential fund-raising juggernaut.

That's because he's been fighting the symptom and not the cause.

Poor Stewardship

The broadcast airwaves are not only the most important communications medium for politics and democracy, they are also a publicly owned asset—like the oceans, the atmosphere and the national forests. Indeed, the airwaves are the most valuable resource of the Information Age, a core ingredient for a variety of emerging, innovative technologies. But broadcasters, who earn huge profits from this public resource, pay the public nothing in return for its use.

In the land of free speech, we have permitted a system of "paid speech" to take hold during political campaigns on the closest thing we have to a public square—our broadcast airwaves. This not only restricts access to our political process, it's also poor stewardship of a precious public asset. For decades we've permitted the broadcast industry to profiteer on our airwaves at the expense of our democracy.

Paul Taylor and Norman Ornstein,
"The Case for Free Air Time: A Broadcast
Spectrum Fee for Campaign Finance Reform,"
New America Foundation, June 2002.

Perhaps he would have fared better if he had sided with Common Cause and other progressive groups that have been clamoring for change not in how candidates raise money to pay for TV, but in how TV charges candidates for the all-important airtime.

Virtually all other democratic nations have a system of free airtime for candidates. And Common Cause makes clear that the price we pay for not having such a system is a (relatively) smooth road for incumbents. The organization reports:

In the 435 races for U.S. Congress in 2000, the typical winner outspent the typical loser by nearly three to one during the campaign, and on Election Day, piled up a victory margin of 70 percent to 30 percent—a landslide. A staggering 98.5 percent of all incumbents seeking reelection were successful.

Actually, McCain did try to make progress on this front in 2003, when he coauthored (with Russ Feingold) the Our Democracy, Our Airwaves Act, which sought to make more airtime available for debates and other programming that gives balanced exposure to candidates. It also called for providing the political parties with up to $750 million in vouchers to hand out to their federal candidates, entitling candidates to acquire media time free of charge.

The bill didn't get very far, but the Campaign Legal Center [CLC] maintains an ongoing grassroots campaign to keep the concept alive. The Our Democracy, Our Airwaves Coalition is stacked with every progressive activist organization you might name, from MoveOn to the Sierra Club. But incumbents make the laws, and this one isn't in their best interest, regardless of the side of the aisle on which they're sitting. The coalition's informational video is voiced by Walter Cronkite who, of all people, must know *that's the way it is.*

A Thin Disguise

Conservatives like to decry free airtime proposals as a violation of the First Amendment. The National Association of Broadcasters takes that tack as well, and sent attorney Cameron DeVore to make the case at the initial meeting of then vice president Al Gore's commission on this topic.

DeVore insisted that government-required free airtime would "run squarely into a First Amendment wall [and] it is impossible to escape the conclusion that a free airtime mandate would be. . . struck down by the courts." He said it would be "an insuperable burden" on government to prove that such a requirement didn't infringe on First Amendment freedoms.

But free speech concerns are a thin disguise for broadcasters and conservatives' knee-jerk support of commerce at any cost. Clearly, providing free airtime doesn't limit speech, it expands it. And, it ensures all candidates speak at the same volume. There's nothing that would stop the fund-raising madness faster than dropping the media cost out of campaign budgets, where TV can suck up more than three-quarters of available funds. When you consider that even hotly contested local races can have budgets starting at $3 million, you can see why TV stations are not jumping on the free airtime idea.

But for the rest of us, there's nothing to lose but lopsided campaigns operating under a universal theme that transcends all real issues and all party boundaries: "Show me the money."

> "We spend a lot of time in our news-
> room covering politics and government,
> but we will not be somebody's free me-
> dia."

Candidates Should Not Be Given Free Airtime

Bob Priddy

Bob Priddy is news director of Missourinet, a news and sports radio network, and former chairman of the Radio Television Digital News Association (RTDNA). In the following viewpoint, Priddy declares that mandating free and equal television and radio airtime to political candidates infringes the free speech rights of the media. The author persists that the editorial decisions of news organizations and journalists cannot be forced to accommodate politicians that are unable to buy airtime. Priddy continues that the idea of free airtime allows the government to decide what appropriate campaign coverage is, reducing broadcasters to secondary status.

As you read, consider the following questions:

1. How is requiring radio broadcasters to give free airtime to candidates counterproductive, in Bob Priddy's opinion?

Bob Priddy, "Free Airtime Is Not the Answer," *Communicator*, December 2004. Reproduced by permission.

2. According to Priddy, what does John McCain fail to demand of politicians seeking free airtime?

3. What kinds of censorship problems arise with free airtime, as stated by the author?

The greatest dangers to liberty lurk in insidious encroachment by men of zeal, well-meaning but without understanding.

—*U.S. Supreme Court Justice Louis Brandeis, 1928*

"Jan?"

"Yes, Bob."

"Could you send a letter to John McCain for me?"

"The senator from Arizona? Why are you sending a memo to a senator from way out there?"

"Because he's threatening to stick his nose right in here. McCain has been threatening broadcasters and their news departments with congressional action if we don't let his kind have free access to our air."

"He can't do that, can he?"

"He sure thinks he can. He waved around a Southern California University study showing that more than half of all of the top-rated local news operations in the country provided no campaign coverage in the seven weeks before the 2002 elections."

"Isn't that bad?"

"Well, it's unfortunate, Jan, because covering politics and government is something that is essential for the news media to do in a free society. But we have consultants running around saying politics and government aren't sexy enough unless sex is involved. They're full of it, of course. They ask inadequate questions, get negative answers, and sell their inadequacies to stations for lots of money. The stations think they have to follow flawed advice because they've paid lots of money for it. . . .

"But that's not the point. The point is, editorial decisions about the content of our newscasts should be left to the editors, not some pol [politician] who can't raise enough money or who can't spend enough money to buy the commercials that wipe out all of the hard work done by stations that *do* cover politics and campaigns. When government starts dictating journalistic decisions, we've lost an important part of our freedoms and a significant value that sets our country apart from others."

Distinctly Un-American

"So what are you going to tell him?"

"I'm going to tell him that although I respect his service to this nation, he is proposing something that is distinctly un-American."

"Un-American! That's a pretty strong message to somebody whose service you say you respect, isn't it?"

"Yeah, but I don't know any better way to put it. It is as un-American for government to dictate to news organizations what they *must* say or what they *must* cover as it is for government to tell reporters they must *not* report some things, and God knows we've got a lot of that going on right now. A lot of people seem to think the phrase 'free press' is less important than 'controlled press,' or 'manipulated press.' Some folks on the FCC [Federal Communications Commission] are saying government might consider free airtime as a factor in license renewals. And one commissioner said the commission is putting broadcasters on notice that they'll be watched."

"Well, don't some broadcasters give free airtime already?"

"Sure. Voluntarily. They do it different ways. But it's *their* decision to do it, and *they* maintain editorial control over the content of those appearances. It's not the government threatening their livelihood if they don't just hand over some free time.

Including Radio, Too

"Another problem, Jan, is that I haven't heard McCain talk about forcing radio to give free time. Radio is a huge part of our communities and our political system. And we have a lot more newscasts than television stations have. Let's face it, when one part of the political spectrum wants to exercise great influence on the public, it's not talk television they use. If he's really serious about forcing exposure of candidates on the public, he should be including radio in his demands.

"But that would be counterproductive to his cause, because there are so many radio stations that a candidate couldn't stop in for his or her five minutes of free airtime on all those stations and still have enough time to beg special interest donors for big bucks to buy self-aggrandizing commercials. And Lord knows we don't want to limit the ability of candidates to put themselves in the debt of people who give them a lot of money so they can air manipulative messages. It's much better, and perhaps more demagogically popular, to blame the media for the shortcomings of the political campaign system than it is to improve the integrity of that system.

"There's nothing new in that philosophy, which is a shame. But we don't often see these characters threatening to destroy a major community source of public information because they don't like the way some information is or is not distributed.

"I have not yet heard McCain demand that people on his side do anything about their own shortcomings. He doesn't plan to require the candidates to be candid and honest in answering questions during their free time. He doesn't want to require straight answers to straight questions. He doesn't want to penalize candidates who use half-truths and innuendo in their public appearances or their commercials. He just wants time from our newscasts without requiring the beneficiaries to be responsible or accurate in their claims about themselves or their opponents.

"And try to imagine a situation like the one we had in Missouri's third congressional district this year. Thirteen candidates were running in the primary for one seat. I looked at the list of candidates for statewide and federal office in the St. Louis area. There were 62 of them. Imagine being a St. Louis TV station trying to give 62 candidates five minutes of free time, each. And they'd all want it during the last week before the election, of course. It won't take much to turn an unrealistic situation into one that's just plain silly.

"I'm sorry a great American like John McCain would propose something as un-American as the government dictating to news departments who is worthy of their time and how they should cover campaigns. We spend a lot of time in our newsroom covering politics and government, but we will not be somebody's free media. We set the agenda for our coverage, not somebody with a special interest or a personal gain to be achieved.

"And what happens if the candidate who is using his mandated free time utters an expletive that the FCC doesn't like? Remember when Barry Commoner ran for president in 1980 and ran commercials that started with the word for cattle excrement? The FCC wouldn't let us censor that commercial. How could we censor someone who is using his or her free time, especially if we are under government orders to let them speak? Or should we risk our licenses and let the expletive go on the air because it says something about the standards of the candidate? The FCC and John [McCain] might have to get together to decide what our marching orders should be, although the thought of those two jointly deciding how much damage they can do to our First Amendment rights is pretty terrifying.

A Penalty of a Free Society

"Maybe we do have a flawed system of covering politics and government. It certainly has its critics, including Senator

"Public Interest" Regulation

As economic history has made clear, "public interest" regulation rarely has much to do with what the viewing public really desires—rather, the public interest theory has been used as a universal excuse for politicians and industry interests to use regulation to achieve a variety of ends. . . . What politicians are perhaps afraid to ask is: Does the public really want to watch more campaign commercials and politically oriented programming and debates, or would they rather tune into *American Idol* or a rerun of *The West Wing?*

Adam Thierer and John Samples,
"The Subsidized Soapbox: Senator McCain's Free Airtime for Politicians Bill," Tech Knowledge, *vol. 55, August 18, 2003.*

McCain. But one of the penalties of a free society relying on free sources of information is the flaws within those sources. When government thinks it can fix those flaws through dictation or prohibition, it is undermining the freedoms that people expect government to protect, not inhibit.

"Here's the big difference between him and me on this issue, Jan. As a free American journalist, I will decide whether a candidate is worthy of a story or time on my newscast. Under his plan, my freedom to make that editorial decision is secondary to his idea that government should be able to demand that I give him that time whether he deserves it or not, whether I've covered his campaign or not. He wants the government to tell me what an acceptable level of campaign coverage is. Simply put, he wants to infringe on the First Amendment. I want to uphold it. And I hope a lot of other news directors do, too.

"Now, he's going to argue that the First Amendment protections don't really apply to broadcast journalists because we use the public airwaves for our reporting. That argument is a fraud. Just because I don't kill trees to circulate my reports does not make me a second-class citizen under the First Amendment. My responsibilities to the public as a journalist are the same as those whose work appears on the printed page. And our protections under the First Amendment should be the same too.

"So, Jan . . . are you ready to start writing that memo?"

"Sure. I didn't know all of this was going on."

"Not many folks in the general public do. And a lot of people in the general public think we're only getting what's coming to us, which is why *we* need to be more public in discussing these issues. Anyway. . . .

"Dear Senator McCain. . . ."

Periodical Bibliography

The following articles have been selected to supplement the diverse views presented in this chapter.

Sharon Begley   "Ready, Aim, Fire!" *Newsweek*, October 11, 2008.

John Heilemann   "The Low-Road Warrior," *New York Magazine*, August 1, 2008.

James Leach   "Negative Political Ads Hurt the United States," *U.S. News & World Report*, October 6, 2008.

David Lightman   "Why Doesn't Negative Campaigning Work Like It Used To?" *McClatchy*, February 22, 2008.

Barbara Lippert   "Attack Ads Lose Their Bite," *Adweek*, November 10, 2008.

Adam Liptak   "Justices Seem Skeptical of Scope of Campaign Law," *New York Times*, March 24, 2009.

Thomas E. Mann   "Suppressing Political Speech?" Brookings Institution, July 9, 2007.

Abby Rapoport   "What's Next for Campaign Finance?" *American Prospect*, July 24, 2008.

Sherry Rauh   "The Psychology of Political Ads," WebMD, October 22, 2008. www.webmd.com.

USA Today   "Our View on the Presidential Campaign: Every Candidate in Every Debate? Fair but a Mistake," July 26, 2007. http://blogs.usatoday.com.

OPPOSING
VIEWPOINTS®
SERIES

CHAPTER 4

What Is the Future
of Advertising?

Chapter Preface

The smartphone has become an advertiser's best friend: It can collect data such as personal information, location, and habits from BlackBerrys, iPhones, and other gadgets to customize mobile ads to the user. "The basic idea is, you go through all these channels, and you get as much data as possible,"[1] says Eswar Priyadarshan, the chief technology officer of Quattro Wireless, a mobile marketing company. Priyadarshan claims that twenty types of information can be gleaned when a customer on Quattro's network surfs the Internet or downloads applications.

Privacy advocates are up in arms over such marketing tactics. "Many of the same consumer data collection, profiling, and behavioral targeting techniques that raise concerns in the more 'traditional' online world have been purposefully migrated into the mobile marketplace,"[2] argues Jeff Chester, executive director of the Center for Digital Democracy. Furthermore, Ed Mierzwinski of U.S. PIRG (Public Interest Research Group) contends, "As the user's location has become part of the data collection and targeting process, the 'mobile marketing ecosystem'—as the industry calls it—poses serious new threats to consumer privacy."[3]

Industry experts, however, propose that mobile marketing can strike a balance with privacy concerns. "The solution is to allow mobile users to opt in to a campaign," suggests Mike Wehrs, president and chief executive officer of the Mobile Marketing Association (MMA). "By opting in, mobile users understand and acknowledge that some information about them and their habits—such as the Web and WAP [wireless application protocol] sites they visit—will be collected and used to send them relevant offers and other information."[4] In the following chapter, the authors discuss how advertising will be shaped by technological innovation and the changing media landscape.

Notes

1. *New York Times*, March 11, 2009. www.nytimes.com.
2. Center for Digital Democracy, January 13, 2009. www.democraticmedia.org.
3. Center for Digital Democracy, January 13, 2009. www.democraticmedia.org.
4. Fierce Mobile Content, September 15, 2009. www.fiercemobilecontent.com.

"The more a media outlet is reliant on ad revenue, the more susceptible it is to failure."

Advertising Is Failing

Douglas Haddow

In the following viewpoint, Douglas Haddow declares that the business of advertising is outmoded and unsustainable. In the age of the Internet, consumers once dependent on the mass media are free to create and consume their own content, he claims, shrinking revenues from advertisements and triggering the industry-wide collapse of magazines and newspapers. The author states that advertising agencies are giving up on repetitive persuasion, buying ad space, and other conventions in favor of promotional tactics that will restore quality content and journalism—or destroy weakened media outlets. A former advertising professional, Haddow is a writer and creative consultant based in Victoria, British Columbia, Canada.

As you read, consider the following questions:

1. How did the 1929 stock market crash affect the advertising industry in 1933, as stated by Douglas Haddow?

Douglas Haddow, "Pop Nihilism: Advertising Eats Itself," *Adbusters*, June 5, 2009. Reproduced by permission of the author.

2. According to the author, how did advertising transform during World War II?

3. What is the significance of Burger King's Facebook promotion, according to Haddow?

Anyone presently employed within this giant glob of microchips, paper, ink and transistor tubes commonly referred to as "the media" knows just how drastic the implications of the recession have become.

Snark blogs are aglow with schadenfreude [pleasure at the misfortune of others] that revels in the desperation spilling forth from the tweets of recent media redundancies. Network television, magazines and newspapers are all under threat because the credit crisis has shaken loose the linchpin that keeps commercial media afloat: advertising.

Penny-pinching, cheeseburger-wolfing consumers are spending less and are enjoying more free online content. That much we all know. As a result, corporate ad budgets have been slashed, setting off a line of collapsing dominoes that is triggering the implosion of mass media.

Soup kitchen lines are filling up with copywriters and journalists alike, and everybody is searching for an answer: a monetary messiah to deliver them from this catastrophe. Amid all the clamor, infighting and vitriol, the following opinion was voiced:

"Advertising is failure."

An innocent, economically structured sentence comprised of two nouns and a verb. But these words will elicit a genuine response from even the most resolute, square-jawed, Glenlivet-sipping adman. He might even let out an unscripted cringe, blush or scoff.

The sentence was articulated by none other than Jeff Jarvis, blogger, *Guardian* columnist and revered media consultant, who qualified it by saying: "If you have a great product or service, customers sell for you . . . you don't need to advertise."

Anyone emotionally invested in advertising will immediately discount the idea that "advertising is failure" as preposterous and asinine. But the logic of "advertising is failure" speaks not only to the quality of a consumer product but [also] precisely to the crisis at hand: the more a media outlet is reliant on ad revenue, the more susceptible it is to failure.

But for many who work within the industry, advertising is not economy- or media-specific. It shouldn't yield to the ebb and flow of the boom/bust cycle. It is a philosophical absolute, a cultural imperative that corresponds to the very core of our being. But for the average Joe and Jane, it is a nuisance, a senseless annoyance and, arguably, one of the key contributors to the financial meltdown.

So what if Jarvis's statement is more pertinent than it is provocative? What if advertising does, at its core, represent some sort of structural failure?

An American Invention

In order to answer this question we need to understand how mass media came to depend on advertising and how we, as citizens of capitalist democracies, came to accept the amount of advertising we consume today as normal.

Modern advertising is primarily an American invention that got its start in early 18th-century newspapers. The first print ads were placed in dailies like the *Boston News-Letter* and the *Virginia Gazette*. The ads were typically text, although some were accompanied by illustrations. The standard ad listed information about new products, property sales or descriptions of runaway slaves and reward details.

It wasn't until after WWI [World War I] that the ad industry came into its own. Following the collapse of 19th-century empires, a progressive middle class began to emerge across the new America. New products were beginning to appear in the marketplace, and a new medium was needed in order to distinguish brands from one and other. Consumerism was a fresh phenomenon. The consumer, pockets flush with money, happily embraced the dawn of modernity and the conveniences of mass consumption.

By the mid-1920s agency copywriters had already figured out how to appeal to the more psychologically complex aspects of consumer choice: Print ads began to prey on the individual's fear of social failure, and radio announcers told tales of how their competitors' products would lead to illness. Unchecked by any sort of regulatory body, advertising agencies had the freedom to pitch whatever worked best. Over the span of just a few years, advertisers successfully convinced the great unwashed to brush their teeth regularly, rinse with mouthwash and smoke as many cigarettes as humanly possible.

The business community was the first to acknowledge advertising's effectiveness, and the industry experienced unprecedented growth. Billboards were erected en masse, and print media was flooded with spurious claims, poetic copy and outlandish promises. The American adman became the vanguard of modernity, molding popular taste and defining trends, as skyscrapers were rapidly erected around his chiseled vision of mass consumption.

Unverified and often absurd pseudoscience became the norm. The Lucky Strike Dance Orchestra was the hottest pop music radio show on the planet, and everybody cheerfully lit up to celebrate the good times. Coca-Cola, previously marketed as a medicinal elixir, began promoting itself as a "fun food."

The economy was booming, and ad agency media purchases allowed magazines, newspapers and radio stations to expand their audience and, in turn, deliver larger markets to advertisers. It was the beginning of a symbiotic relationship between advertising and media.

Ad Nauseam

These were the halcyon days of the American oligarchy, when business interests trumped all facets of communications and government. Indebted to ad revenue, the news media [were] quick to adopt the values of the corporations they promoted. But as more ads started to pop up, marketing a wide variety of superfluous products under terms ranging from vague to vulgar, a grassroots anti-advertising movement began to percolate across the nation. Advertising was, after all, still a novel force in the public consciousness.

In 1927 *Your Money's Worth: A Study in the Waste of the Consumer's Dollar* by Stuart Chase and F.J. Schlink became a best seller within weeks of publication. The authors' take on the nature of advertising sent shockwaves of alarm through the burgeoning advertising establishment.

> "Consider the sheer superfluity of certain kinds of goods which this forcing of turnover entails. We are deluged with things which we do not wear, which we lose, which go out of style, which make unwelcome presents for our friends, which disappear anyhow—fountain pens, cigar lighters, cheap jewelry, patent pencils, mouthwashes, key rings, Mahjong sets, automobile accessories—endless jiggers and doodads and contrivances. Here the advertiser plays on the essential monkey within us, and uses up mountains of good iron ore and countless sturdy horsepower to fill—a few months later—the wagon of the junkman."

On the eve of the 1929 stock market crash, ad spending had inflated up to three-and-a-half billion dollars per year, cementing the adman's place as the defining force in American culture. But on the morning of Black Tuesday, as police began to clean up the freshly splattered corpses wrought by the panic of economic collapse, the adman's fortunes took a profound turn for the worse.

The crash triggered an abrupt decline across the board and the industry lost more than half its revenue by 1933. The crash also served to catalyze the emerging anti-advertising movement. Thinkers like Chase and Schlink developed a scientific approach to combating deceptive advertising and urged the public and government to take a critical stance against the promotion of overconsumption. Militant consumer organizations sprang up, and people from all walks of life came together and formed a broad voice to contest Wall Street and Madison Avenue's [New York City street that is synonymous with the advertising industry] collective failure.

Around the same time, Dell Publishing launched *Ballyhoo* magazine, which lampooned the gaudy and obnoxious nature of the roaring '20s advertising style. The first issue of *Ballyhoo*, which contained no ads, sold 120,000 copies in just two days. The parody mag reached a circulation of one-and-a-half million within its first five months. Coinciding with the popular outrage toward America's ad nauseam, *Ballyhoo* made a mockery of the industry and its shill.

A deepening public distrust, coupled with the fear that advertising had become nothing more than a big joke to the average consumer, compelled industry leaders to lash out at its critics. Ad execs mobilized expensive PR [public relations] campaigns and accused the movement's key figures of being Communist and anti-American. The debate raged throughout the [Great] Depression, culminating in the passing of laws such as the Wheeler-Lea Act, which limited the amount of deception an agency could inject into its ad spots.

Brand America

The industry's public image was in tatters, and the adman's ability to persuade had been significantly subverted. It seemed as if it was only going to get worse, but then, out of thin air, a stroke of luck: The Japanese sneak attack on Pearl Harbor thrust America into World War II. The downtrodden suits of Madison Avenue saw nothing but a silver lining to the dark clouds that surrounded the Hawaiian islands.

Strategy-minded admen capitalized on the war as an opportunity to market their industry as a force for good to both the government and the public. Agency heads argued that advertising was a "keystone of American values" and that any attacks leveled against it were synonymous with enemy sentiment. The war wasn't just a battle between the Axis and Allies, it encapsulated a broader struggle between totalitarianism and all-American free enterprise.

Immediately after the United States joined the war, leading agencies grouped together and offered their services, free of charge, to the domestic information program. The War Advertising Council was created in March of 1942, and the agencies involved contributed more than 100 campaigns to the war effort at an estimated cost of one billion dollars. Posters depicting consumer splendor were stripped down and replaced with paranoid and patriotic pleas for money and stern requests for hard work and self-control on behalf of the nation. Slogans like "Rationing Gives You Your Fair Share" and "To Dress Extravagantly in War Time is Unpatriotic" dotted city streets. A medium that just a year before had become a laughingstock was now the primary codifier of moral behavior.

And with that the anti-advertising movement was sabotaged and rendered anti-American. The Marlboro-smoking GI [a member of the armed forces] had defeated the face of evil, and through the destruction of their enemies, America embraced the pro-corporate "brand America" peddled to the public by the same minds who sold them their war bonds. Through four years of effective propaganda campaigning, agency luminaries were able to position their medium as an acceptable form of persuasion, and anyone who contested its legitimacy was labeled pinko [derogatory term for a Communist sympathizer who is not a member of the Communist Party] scum.

The last major attempt to derail the advancement of advertising's predominance was made by former adman turned academic William Benton in 1945.

Benton proposed that the Federal Communications Commission (FCC) establish a number of ad-free, subscription-based radio stations to compete with ad-funded commercial stations. He argued that advertising was destroying the quality of on-air content and that this would be more in tune with the American spirit of competition. Benton's proposal was denounced by the likes of the *New York Times*, NBC and CBS who alleged that it was "undemocratic." The proposal, however, was withdrawn before it could be approved, as Benton accepted the position of assistant secretary of state with the US government. Admen everywhere breathed a sigh of relief.

The Golden Age of Advertising

The era from 1945 onwards came to be known as "the golden age of advertising." Upon repatriation, the battle-weathered GI—always with a smoke in hand, was transformed into Leo Burnett's Marlboro Man—a big idea straight from the subconscious of the Old West. Patriotic and masculine, the iconic cowboy with a longhorn hanging from his lip was plastered onto billboards far and wide across the great American landscape: road signs pointing the consumer toward utopia on a highway with no end.

By 1964, just 19 years after the Nazis disbanded, [Adolf] Hitler's Volkswagen became a hit with the hip, freewheeling youth, thanks to a minimalist campaign that presented the "people's car" as a revolutionary vehicle for a new generation of automobile consumers.

Ad agencies had mastered the ability to sell the American consumer products that they had never heard of and had no real need for. This was the cunning genius of advertising. In the words of David Ogilvy, perhaps the most successful adman of all time:

"I do not regard advertising as entertainment or an art form, but as a medium of information. When I write an advertisement, I don't want you to tell me that you find it 'creative.' I want you to find it so interesting that you buy the product."

And buy the product we did. The jaws of Western civilization became unhinged and with advertising defining our desires, we let four decades of plastic-wrapped "new" slide down our collective gullet. From Cool Whip to custom cheeseburgers, Ogilvy's philosophy of the "big idea"—and its myriad bastardizations—served as the blueprint for the mechanisms our entire socioeconomic machinery grew to depend on.

That is, until it failed . . . again.

Like an unsavory remake of a classic Hollywood blockbuster, the drama of 1929 is being rerun right before our eyes: Main Street is broke, Wall Street is the villain, and Madison Avenue is in crisis.

But here's the twist: In 1929 mass media and its offshoot, the mass market, were just coming into existence. In 2009 we're seeing the first major signals of their collapse.

The Consumer Controls Everything

In the new media environment, the consumer is bound by nothing and controls everything. We've crept out of the living room—away from the creature comforts of four-channel nuclear families, vacuum tubes and TV dinners—into the vast, dark wilderness of the Internet. We've become roving vagabonds and pirates who create media just as easily as we consume and dispense with it.

The anti-advertising hostility that broke out during the [Great] Depression has reemerged, this time as a passive dismissal. Rather than spending thousands of hours working to form a grassroots revolution, all we need now is a simple wave of the hand or a twitch of the finger to negate the pervasive gawp of the ad biz.

The Antithesis of Good Design

Advertising at its worst, at the peak of its hubris, was the antithesis of good design. There are more than one parallel to be made to the record industry, aside from the fact that their inability to control this new media is what has led to their undoing. Both were, in their heyday, purely profit driven, with little to no interest in what the consumer actually wanted (because we'll tell you what you want, thank you very much), and little to no investment in creating a better product. Both have become massive, bloated, impossibly wealthy, and both have had their best days behind them.

Ryan McManus,
"The End of Advertising, and Why We Should Celebrate,"
Barbarian Blog, April 23, 2008. www.barbariangroup.com.

This is a direct assault on the power of advertising, which is rooted in force and persuasion. In the past, if you wanted to consume media you were forced to deal with advertising's attempts to persuade. But as cities begin to shed their billboards in favor of cleaner aesthetics (São Paulo, Xi'an, Quebec City), and we move from ad-saturated commercial media to the laptop, attempts at coercion are in vain. Unlike the television viewer, the Internet user has been conditioned to distrust online advertising from the beginning, due to its association with viruses and overall desktop dysfunction.

Not only have these shifts in how we consume media undermined the effectiveness of advertising, the industry itself has given up on its traditional models in pursuit of an abstract preoccupation with "creativity." While the word "creative" has long served as advertising rhetoric, it wasn't until recently that the industry's ability to self-promote eclipsed its natural repellant, and ad agencies became desirable employers for young creatives.

George Orwell once said, "Advertising is the rattling of a stick inside a swill bucket." But due to the work of agencies like Wieden+Kennedy or Crispin Porter + Bogusky (CP+B), such statements simply don't speak to today's creative twenty-somethings, who see advertising as a pure venue for their ability.

But creativity is not a force that you can use to schlep superfluous objects to uninterested consumers—that requires repetition, persuasion and the power of mass media. True creativity is inherently destructive, and truly creative individuals always, without exception, seek to destroy the mediums they work within.

Pop Nihilists

With the influx of creatives into the industry, agencies have opened their doors to an intellectual insurgency, every innovation pushing the medium closer to the edge. This is the essence of Joseph Schumpeter's "creative destruction" save one critical difference: Rather than supplanting outdated companies, the creative destructionists of advertising will force their medium into oblivion. This is the birth of advertising's Dada era.

If Ogilvy were alive, he would surely be cursing today's creatives as nihilists: young Turks [radicals] hell-bent on annihilating the nobility of a medium that defined consumer civilization for the greater part of the last century. They are nihilistic not only because they seek to destroy the meaning of advertising but also because they believe that good advertising need not be a force of repetition, that it can bring about popularity through quality content alone.

These "pop nihilists" don't want to sell boring shit to an emaciated class of brain-dead plebs [plebeians; common people]—they want to create engaging content that inspires dialog between individuals and the brands they connect with, and they want to do it in an interesting, artful manner that doesn't insult your intelligence.

While this position overlooks the inane bleakness of what "brand dialog" says about those who engage in it and the inherently destructive nature of consumer capitalism, it is nonetheless an abrupt departure from advertising's traditional function: repetitive persuasion. And this is where the scruffy, blog-brained twentysomething creative begins to take on the profile of a saboteur.

Radical creatives who have entered the industry within the last few years tend to have little or no faith in the viability of "BDAs" (big dumb agencies). They view the established order as antiquated and staffed by frauds and has-beens, old-media curmudgeons who still watch television and don't take the remix revolution seriously.

They acknowledge that advertising has been outmoded by Google, PR, and social media and is now becoming irrelevant to both the client and the consumer. In an age where we can instantly access the resources we need, attempts by advertisers to obnoxiously force brand presence into our lives comes off as a desperation tactic.

This abrupt shift in thinking has caused ad agencies to divide along demographic lines—those favoring the mass market and traditional client service, versus progressive creative agencies that embrace chaos. The former will die a death of natural causes, going the way of the Betamax, becoming little more than landfill like the Walkmans and Furbies of yore. On the other hand, the creatives will segue into a situation that can best be described as cannibalistic.

Case in point: recent Burger King campaigns by industry leader CP+B. The firm has executed a string of inflammatory television and Web spots involving Burger King that has caused an uproar within the blogosphere and traditional news media, generating millions of dollars of free PR for their client.

One such campaign, "Whopper Sacrifice"—in which Facebook users were rewarded a free Whopper for deleting ten friends from their account—has been the most precise incidence of "pop nihilism" to date. The underlying premise of the campaign was that the majority of one's relationships are expendable, the Whopper serving as a material excuse to manifest this belief. The Whopper's presence in the campaign was purely symbolic. The true appeal of the sacrifice was not the faux-nourishment of a hamburger, but for participants to relish in the misanthropic destruction of the social contract.

These campaigns are intentionally polemic—eliciting disgust in many, while others feel compelled to come to their defense. CP+B have torn a page right out of *Ballyhoo* in the sense that they aren't selling hamburgers, they are selling the spectacle of advertising's demise. Agencies who take this route and profit from its fleeting popularity will go down in history as advertising's robber barons, those who cashed in on the medium's social capital before it went bankrupt—signifying the moment advertising realized its own mortality and began to eat itself.

As the industry nears its 100,000th post-recession layoff, dragging newspapers, magazines and television down with it, it's become apparent that selling ad space is an unsustainable revenue model for media as a whole. It is from the chaos of this moment that the relationship between content and capital will be defined for generations to come. Either quality content and valuable journalism will prevail, or a failing ad industry will survive by cannibalizing faltering media outlets: pitting the sponsored versus the authentic in a death match for attention, relevance and the almighty dollar.

| *"Search marketing has breathed new life into online advertising."*

The Future of Advertising Is the Internet

Alison Overholt

Alison Overholt is a staff writer for Fast Company, *an entrepreneurial magazine. In the following viewpoint, Overholt affirms that advertising has great potential to consumers using Internet search engines to find products and services. Troubleshooting for bugs is inevitable in these new types of advertisements, but she speculates that they may become as common as the thirty-second commercial. Overholt advises businesses and marketers to use three techniques in creating text- and search-related ads: (1) keep them in context with online content, (2) analyze the online behavior of consumers, and (3) provide information on where consumers can buy the products or services locally.*

As you read, consider the following questions:

1. What is the main objective of the search engine marketing industry, as stated by Alison Overholt?

Alison Overholt, "Search for Tomorrow," *Fast Company*, December 19, 2007. Republished with permission of Fast Company, conveyed through Copyright Clearance Center, Inc.

2. Why are publishers reluctant of contextual online ads, according to Overholt?

3. How does Lance Podell respond to privacy concerns of tracking customers online?

It was an advertiser's worst nightmare. Last summer [2006], the *New York Post* ran a breathless story about a gruesome murder in which the victim's body was hacked to pieces, the parts stashed in an old suitcase. Opposite the online version of the story ran an advertisement cheerily touting the benefits of . . . luggage.

The offending ad was served up using Google's search marketing technology called AdWords. For the uninitiated, search engine marketing lets advertisers bid on keywords or phrases. Top bidders then have their ads appear alongside search results whenever a user types in that phrase. Or in this case, the ads run alongside editorial content containing the keywords. Suitcase in the article. Suitcase ad. We have a match.

It was an excruciating goof, emblematic of the tricky juncture where the search engine marketing industry finds itself today: The dream is to transform the Internet into a sales tool that finally delivers on the promise to generate eminently qualified, targeted, and trackable customer leads that convert quickly into big sales. Marketers that embraced the first generation of these tools have already achieved phenomenal success by targeting ads to consumers seeking products and services on search engines. Now the toolmakers, predominantly Google and Yahoo!, want to serve up ads to the rest of the Web—delivering relevant messages not just when buyers come to a search engine already hunting for something, but any time, and any place.

There's big money at stake in nailing the solution. In an advertising environment that has steadily weakened over the past three years, search marketing has breathed new life into online advertising by showing how powerful it can be when an advertiser catches a shopper's attention at that perfect moment when she is ready to buy.

Advertisers rewarded the nascent industry by doubling its revenues in 2003 to the tune of $1.9 billion (a figure that is expected to jump again in 2004 to $2.8 billion dollars, says Forrester Research), or nearly one-third of all online advertising spending. And those hefty totals ring up in small increments: Expedia, for example, is the top bidder on Yahoo!'s service for "Miami vacation," paying 83 cents a lead.

Three techniques are emerging that could push online ad revenues even higher: contextual ads, behavioral ads, and local ads. But none of them are slam dunks. In pushing the envelope to make related text ads as ubiquitous as the 30-second TV spot, the search engines and the marketers that use them tap-dance along a very fine line between what is helpful and what is obnoxious, what is exciting and what is simply in very poor taste.

Keeping Things in Context

"We advertise on TV and radio," says Steve Hartmann, the director of online marketing for eHarmony, an online dating service. "But we discovered that a lot of people only vaguely remember our name. Maybe they'd just catch the word 'harmony' and that we were a dating service. When they typed that in at a search site, that's when they'd find us." Hartmann discovered that close to 70% of eHarmony's new customers from online advertising channels arrive through search-based ads.

Seeking to go to the next level, Hartmann bought contextual ads from both Google and Overture (owned by Yahoo!). He did so because the ability to place eHarmony ads where serious-minded singles spend time on the Web—say reading an article on CNN's Web site about a scientific discovery on the brain chemistry of love—sounded ideal. Google and Overture dominate search marketing and offer contextual ads through partners such as AOL, MSN, CNN.com, and the Web sites of the *New York Times* and the *Washington Post*.

But contextual ads don't seem to target consumers as effectively as pure search ads. "We're definitely not seeing the traffic from newspaper sites that we see with search engines," Hartmann says.

There are many reasons for this lower success rate. Many publishers are leery of these ads for fear of blurring the lines between editorial and advertising, so their reach is limited. The bugs in the system also remain, ergo the very targeted but terribly unfortunate luggage ad. These incidents expose the flaw in the logic that purchasing a given keyword can guarantee relevancy to the material next to the ad.

Overture has responded by instituting an editorial review process. "We needed human influence to deal with those words that are ambiguous in meaning," says David Karnstedt, senior vice president and general manager of direct business at Overture. Google, meanwhile, believes its technology can fix any editorial problems.

Perhaps more problematic to contextual marketing's prospects is the very nature of the Internet experience. When someone types the name of a product or service into a search engine, chances are he wants to find it and buy it. When that same person surfs a news or content site, he may just be catching up on the day's events. "They're not in shopping mode, they're in browsing mode," says Danny Sullivan, an analyst who runs SearchEngineWatch.com. And there's not any fine-tuning that can be done to fix that.

Fresh Ads for Good Behavior

Because of the inherent flaws in contextual marketing online, the stakes are even higher for the online advertising industry's next big play: behavioral marketing. This technique promises to serve up ads based on a Web surfer's habits and mind-set. "You're targeting the person, not the content," says Forrester

All Over the Internet

On the Internet, too, advertisers are finding more ways to intertwine marketing messages with entertainment. Online travel agency Orbitz has managed to entice Web surfers to bask in its marketing messages by embedding them in online pop-up ads built around simple interactive sports-themed games like Sink the Putt. Not only that, but players who like the games often forward links to them to friends and colleagues, spreading the message at no extra cost to Orbitz. LiveVault, a Marlborough, Mass., data back-up and recovery provider, got the same sort of free ride when it produced and released on the Web a short comic video about backing up data, starring [British actor] John Cleese. LiveVault CEO [chief executive officer] Bob Cramer claims the $500,000 price tag for the video promotion was a bargain, given the big response. "It ended up all over the Internet," he gloats.

David H. Freeman,
"The Future of Advertising Is Here," Inc.com,
August 1, 2005. www.inc.com.

analyst Charlene Li. It's far more ambitious—and more advertiser-friendly—than contextual marketing. "You could never target intent before, in any medium," says Li, capturing what's exciting about the new method. "You just put your message out there around content that seemed likely to attract the right people and hoped it worked."

To deliver on that opportunity is a daunting technological task. It requires analyzing the surfing habits of millions of users in order to define segments based on what users are reading, how often they read it, and what products they search for. One of the first entrants in the market is Kanoodle, a small

New York-based search marketing firm. It has joined with on-line advertising network 24/7 Real Media to launch Behavior-Target, a behavioral search service. "We've created a taxonomy of 486 topics that we'll roll out slowly as we reach critical mass with each audience segment," explains David Hill, president of media solutions at 24/7 Real Media. "If you visit sports sites several times a month and fashion sites several times a month, you might fall within our 'active women' behavioral segment." Unless you're a guy who likes sports *and* fashion, or works in one of those industries.

Though a potential gold mine for advertisers, data collection on this scale—and at this level of detail—is, for many consumers, a little scary. It raises a host of privacy issues as well as questions about who retains the rights to or ownership of particular kinds of information. Lance Podell, president of Kanoodle, is quick to defend his company's concern for privacy. "I'm tracking a cookie, not you, and you will be able to opt out at any time. That cookie doesn't know your address or your Social Security number, it just knows your behavior. IP [Internet Protocol] addresses aren't being collected," he says.

Lycos is one of the first companies to sign up for BehaviorTarget. Says Steve Gross, Lycos's vice president of marketing, "We need different and creative ways of making money off of our user base. We have a unique user base in the tens of millions, but our ability to understand that base was limited." Consider a group of users who have been defined as car enthusiasts because they visit automotive sites such as Edmunds.com and NASCAR.com. Gross is eager to sell ads aimed at that group and deliver marketing messages to them even when they're visiting a technology blog. "Television advertisers would love to understand composition this well, to identify audiences and what they want, beyond just age and sex, which is how they sell ads now," says Hill.

So although it may seem simplistic to get lumped into a bucket because of a few Web-surfing habits, it is better information, as Gross notes, than most advertisers have to work with. Yet even its boosters acknowledge that behavioral marketing is a work in progress. "There are things we're still working out," admits Hill. "For example, somebody goes to a series of auto sites, but how many times must they visit before they become part of that segment? Our plan is to use our software to watch their behavior over the course of time, then do branding studies to hopefully get the mix and the formula right." If that works, and if the privacy guardians don't howl too loudly, this may be the method with the best chance of taking off.

Think Local, Act Local

If the search engines have learned anything from their original keyword-advertising system, it's that when people type a product name into the search window, they want to buy that product now. Chances are, though, that users see ads from online retailers who can ship it within the week, not the minute. How can you feed immediate needs, such as where's the closest party goods supply store that's open late? Hit 'em where they live.

In March 2004, Google launched a beta site called Local .google.com that lets users search by zip code or local address. Thirty percent of all advertising is purchased in local markets, and the Yellow Pages ad market is estimated at $14 billion per year—a stash that Google would love to break into. So far, the company has focused on importing Yellow Pages data into its local engine and getting the location algorithms right, without serving up additional ads alongside search results. The big question will be whether the advertisers arrive when local goes live.

Seth Berkowitz, vice president of business development at the car-buying information site Edmunds.com, says no thanks. In theory, he's a likely customer, since he sells customer leads to local auto dealers. But he's focusing on buying location-specific keywords through traditional search marketing products. "I love it when people type in 'Los Angeles Honda Dealers' because 20% of those people execute on those ads," he says.

"To make local search work," says Jupiter research analyst Gary Stein, "you have to get all the plumbers and dentists on there, then you have to get people to shift over to thinking about using Google to find plumbers." Don't expect local search to be a significant moneymaker for anyone until national retailers hop on board to let you know where the closest Home Depot is and whether they have that sander in stock you're itching to buy.

It's obviously too early to pass judgment on any of these emerging online marketing techniques, although each has significant flaws. Remember that GoTo.com, the precursor to Overture, was laughed at in its early days for selling simple keywords on a search engine. No matter which, if any, succeed, what's clear is that these models for segmenting, targeting, and reaching customers are forever changing the way companies think about advertising as a sales tool. When you can select your target customer by geography, actual (not projected) buying patterns, and browsing behaviors—and track the return on investment of each ad by following a customer from the time she is targeted to the time she makes the purchase—it's hard to go back to fuzzy math and schmoozy ad salespeople. The technocrats will have the last laugh, even if it's at the marketers' expense.

| "Welcome to the next generation of product placement."

Product Placement Is Becoming More Sophisticated

Brian Stelter

Brian Stelter is a television and digital media reporter for the New York Times. In the following viewpoint, Stelter writes that product placement is becoming more elaborate in TV shows, reality series, and even the news. Because of home-recording technologies that allow viewers to skip commercials, the author contends that advertisers now work with writers, producers, and networks to insert their products into scripts and story lines rather than as props. Stelter contends that critics worry such product placement will lead to uncontrolled commercialization. He proposes that the practice is gaining acceptance and harkens back to corporate-sponsored soap operas and variety shows.

As you read, consider the following questions:

1. What is a "live commercial," as stated by Brian Stelter?

2. What contributed to the rise of the TV commercial, according to Stelter?

Brian Stelter, "Is It a Show or a Commercial?" *New York Times Upfront*, vol. 141, May 4, 2009, p. 20(7). Copyright © 2009 Scholastic Inc. Reprinted by permission of Scholastic Inc.

3. What does David Kaplan say about the consumer response to more sophisticated product placement?

On *Harlem Heights*, a new reality show on BET [Black Entertainment Television], the young stars swish Listerine,
treat their allergies with Zyrtec, and sweeten their coffee with
Splenda.

The products were placed within the scenes of *Harlem
Heights* as part of a deal between Johnson & Johnson, the
company that makes all three products, and cable channel
BET. Through the arrangement, Listerine, Zyrtec, and Ambi
skin care products are woven into the stories of the eight
young New York professionals who are profiled on *Harlem
Heights*; in addition, Splenda and the hand sanitizer Purell are
readily available as the cast go about their daily lives.

Welcome to the next generation of product placement:
Brands of sodas, cars, and mouthwash are no longer just occasional props on TV shows and movies, as they were until
about five years ago [2004]. Now, as part of more elaborate
marketing deals, advertisers are increasingly working with
writers, producers, and the networks to incorporate products
into the story lines of both scripted and reality shows. Even
news shows are doing it, raising difficult questions about journalistic integrity.

Examples are everywhere. Last spring, the characters on
CSI: NY gathered around videoconferencing screens, ostensi-
bly to share information about a shooting, but really to promote Cisco Systems' TelePresence videoconferencing system.
In February, characters on the ABC soap *One Life to Live*
spent the month talking up the health benefits of Campbell's
soups.

In the past year, MTV has produced a series of commercials for its advertisers that look like shows. For example, a
short chase movie called *Get Moe* was actually a series of 60-
second commercials for Mountain Dew. A series of shorts

called *Men of Action* thrust the heroes into violent confrontations that somehow promoted the virtues of KFC and Kay Jewelers.

Fast Forward

One "new" type of ad—a live commercial within a show—is actually a throwback to the early days of TV. Two late-night shows—*The Tonight Show with Jay Leno* and *Jimmy Kimmel Live!*—have recently experimented with live commercials. Leno simply lent his star power by introducing the ad (for Klondike bars), but Kimmel and his sidekick actually do the live ads themselves (for Nikon, Pontiac, and Quiznos), transforming the commercials into comedy skits.

Companies are turning to more sophisticated kinds of product placement on television because they're worried that viewers are no longer paying attention to their ads. TiVo and other DVRs [digital video recorders], which let viewers fast-forward through commercials, are the primary culprits.

About a third of U.S. households—some 30 million—currently have DVRs, but those numbers are likely to rise quickly with the changeover to all-digital broadcasting this year and the increasing number of cable and phone companies offering DVRs as part of their packages. That means millions more viewers will be able to skip right past the 30-second commercials that have long been the backbone of television's economic model.

Advertisers are scrambling to adapt, and more sophisticated product placements are one of the ways to get viewers' attention. Some companies are cutting their conventional ad budgets to put more money into product placement deals; spending on product placement in the United States grew by a third last year.

"We want to blur the lines between the commercial breaks and the entertainment content," says Dario Spina, who handles "integrated marketing" for MTV's entertainment channels like Comedy Central and Spike.

Some creators of TV shows and watchdog groups worry that "branded entertainment" could turn television characters into product promoters instead of storytellers.

It's a "a huge, out-of-control issue," says Robert Weissman of Commercial Alert, a nonprofit group that aims to limit commercial marketing. He says the involvement of advertisers in the shaping of scripts and plots represents "fundamental encroachments on the independence of the programming."

News Shows

The Federal Communications Commission (FCC) has similar concerns, and is considering rules that would require broadcasters to clearly disclose product placements—not just flash them across the screen at the speed of light, which is the current practice.

"We're not saying they can't do it—we're just saying they have to let the audience know what they're doing," says Jonathan S. Adelstein, an FCC commissioner.

Product placement has even found a home on news programs. Last summer, a Fox affiliate in Las Vegas raised alarms when it agreed to a product placement deal with McDonald's. For several weeks, anchors on its morning news show had cups of McDonald's iced coffee on their desks (though they rarely touched the cups). The CBS stations in Hartford, Conn., and Atlanta have also accepted product placements on their morning shows, fueling the debate over potential conflicts of interest.

Others question whether it even works. "In the end, they just make the audiences even more skeptical of everything," says Herbert Jack Rotfeld, a professor of marketing at Auburn University in Alabama.

TV's Early Days

In some ways, this newfangled form of branded entertainment recalls the beginnings of television. Half a century ago, adver-

A Small Percentage

The lingering impediment is that nobody knows precisely where the audience's "ick" factor is but most evidence suggests that they're pretty understanding. According to research from Knowledge Networks, a small percentage of viewers object to product integration, a few actually enjoy it, and the lion's share don't care.

Brian Lowry,
"But First, This Word from Your Anchor. . ."
Variety, vol. 413, no. 1, November 17, 2008.

tisers themselves often produced shows like *The Colgate Comedy Hour* and *Texaco Star Theater,* in which a chorus line of well-dressed gas station attendants opened each show by singing the Texaco jingle ("We're the men of Texaco, we work from Maine to Mexico") before introducing the host, Milton Berle. In fact, "soap operas" got their name because they were so closely associated with their sponsors, soap and detergent manufacturers like Procter & Gamble and Colgate-Palmolive.

News shows were also in on the act. Today, it's called *NBC Nightly News with Brian Williams,* but until 1956, it was the *Camel News Caravan* or the *Plymouth News Caravan,* depending on whether the cigarette maker or the car company was the sponsor that night.

A combination of rising production costs and the quiz show scandals of the late 1950s pushed sponsors out of the business of producing shows themselves. Coming up with new ways to reach consumers, commercial ad spots as we know them today were born.

But products gradually (and subtly) found their way back into TV shows. Hoping that Hollywood's glamour would rub off on their everyday products, companies bartered their wares to producers, giving free props in exchange for the on-screen exposure. It meant extra revenue for the networks, and in a way, made the shows feel more real life.

Then, about eight years ago, product placement became much more intense, partly because of the success of *Survivor*. The show's producer sold sponsorships to advertisers—including Reebok, Ericsson, and Dr. Scholl's—who each paid $4 million to insert their products into the show.

The sponsorship revenue covered most of the show's production costs, which meant CBS could put *Survivor* on the air without any real financial risk. And because success in television always spawns swarms of imitators, the networks latched onto this low-cost programming model.

The result? Reality shows started clogging the networks. They were cheap to produce, popular with viewers—and tailor-made for product placement deals.

In 2008, more than 90,000 product placements appeared on the six broadcast networks, up 6 percent from the previous year, according to the Nielsen Company. *The Biggest Loser* on NBC topped the list of shows with the most product placements, with 6,804.

Taking their cue from the success of the product placement model, philanthropic foundations have recently begun paying networks to weave social messages into TV programs. Call it "message placement": Instead of selling soda or cars, they promote education and healthy living.

This past year, the Bill & Melinda Gates Foundation helped shape story lines and insert messages on stopping the spread of infectious diseases and surgical safety into popular TV shows like *ER*, *Law & Order: Special Victims Unit*, and *Private Practice*.

"There's a lot of research that shows that when a character in a series says, 'I'm going to be an organ donor,' it's effective, more effective than giving out a pamphlet," says Martin Kaplan of the Norman Lear Center at the University of Southern California's Annenberg School for Communication [& Journalism].

As the number of product placements continues to increase, industry analysts say the practice is becoming more and more accepted.

Savvy Viewers

"We haven't seen any noteworthy backlash on the consumer side about product placement," says David Kaplan at Nielsen. "Consumers get that this is part-and-parcel with their television viewing experience these days."

Maybe that's because viewers have become pretty savvy about product placements: Does anyone really wonder why Simon Cowell has a huge Coke [Coca-Cola] cup in front of him on every American Idol?

"I think that most people in the United States know that there's some financial arrangement there," says Ambar Rao, a marketing professor at Washington University in St. Louis.

Tom Meyer, the president of a leading Los Angeles brand management company, agrees.

"These shows have always been funded by advertising," he says, "and if advertising is changing, it has to be understood that the mechanics of how we deliver advertising must change, or advertisers will walk away."

> "Just because sponsored programming is in some sense a return of an old formula doesn't mean it's unworthy of scrutiny."

Product Placement Is Becoming Too Ubiquitous

Alicia Rebensdorf

In the following viewpoint, Alicia Rebensdorf announces that product placement is making a pervasive return to television and radio advertising. Whereas corporate sponsorships and plugs marked the days of early broadcasting, Rebensdorf insists that current techniques of "product integration" lower the aesthetic value of many programs. Furthermore, she alleges that on-air chat and banter inserted with stealth endorsements for brands or services place corporate disclosure into question and threaten consumer choice. Rebensdorf is a writer based in New York City and author of Chick Flick Road Kill: A Behind the Scenes Odyssey into Movie-Made America.

As you read, consider the following questions:

1. What examples of product placement "gone too far" does Alicia Rebensdorf provide?

Alicia Rebensdorf, "Has Product Placement Made Our Television Viewing Experience Worse?" *AlterNet*, May 19, 2007. Reproduced by permission.

2. What is the standard argument against product placement, in Rebensdorf's view?

3. In the author's opinion, what advertising alternatives do the Internet and digital media offer?

It's not news that, in a world of TiVo and YouTube, remote control and cable radio, the traditional commercial is something passé. As standard ads shrink from 30-second slots to 10-second reminders, TV cameras increasingly linger over Survivors [contestants on the reality show *Survivor*] eating Doritos and Jack Bauer [character from television show *24*] driving his Ford on the car company's favorite station FOX. A study last year [2006] discovered that nearly 11 percent of all network minutes include a branded reference and the Philly [*Philadelphia Inquirer*] recently started carrying a Citizens Bank-sponsored column. Last month [April 2006], a Dallas radio station decided to do one better. It pulled ads altogether, replacing them with sponsored segments and product-plugged banter:

> "You know, the best way to get down to Austin for South by Southwest is Southwest Airlines. They have tons of flights. It's the way I travel."

Yes, this so-called "product integration" is all the rage. But by replacing 15 minutes of commercial airtime with two minutes of branded chat, the Clear Channel station, KZPS, did more than prove that what works for *American Idol* can work for radio. It also paraded its announcement as a consumer victory. They claimed their new format both cut down on commercial clutter and marked a return to the golden years of American radio.

"In a sense, we're recapturing the early days of FM," said programmer Duane Doherty, "when your jock [disc jockey] was a trusted guide through what was new and important."

Never mind, for a minute, the use of the terms "trusted" and "important." Doherty has a point. Because direct advertising was not allowed, early radio was always brought to us by our favorite corporate sponsor. *Amos 'n Andy* made Pepsodent toothpaste a household name, and the first TV shows followed the model with *Kraft Hours* and *Camel Newsreels*. But let's not confuse nostalgia for progress. Just because sponsored programming is in some sense a return of an old formula doesn't mean it's unworthy of scrutiny.

A Marketing Euphemism

I'll be honest: I hesitate here. To continue this line of reasoning, to champion the separation of branding and broadcasting feels equally idealistic and hopeless. Product integration—a marketing euphemism that oddly equates advertising techniques with schools in Little Rock—is already too far gone. Most of our sporting venues are now named after beers and banks, and the trend is spreading to schools. News shows' health segments are often bookended by medicinal brand logos, and that Philly newspaper column is most likely just the first. If we are talking radio, on-air personalities have been voicing over car insurance and weight loss plans for years. As evidenced by last year's study of record companies and radio, even the content of most commercial airtime is bought. How do you argue with ads being inserted into commercial programming?

Plus, it's not like Ryan Seacrest [television host] is any Edward Murrow [American broadcast journalist]. Or that media consumers are naïve victims. Most people tuning into FOX generally do so with the understanding that they are watching a certain point of view. And if the stars of their prime-time dramas on that same station all happen to drive the same car make, what real harm is done? We always, after all, have the choice not to watch. Our decision not to opt out of commercial media can be understood as an implicit acceptance of whatever advertising is embedded within.

In response, the standard social critique against product integration—that ad creep feeds a culture of consumption, that it compromises artistic freedom and erodes consumer choice—can seem vague and, considering much of this integrated advertising looks a lot like it did in the '50s, ironically old-fashioned. To argue against other product placement feels like fighting back the climate crisis tide. It feels like preaching abstinence to a couple already in the act.

In fact, the best arguments against product integration seem to be on aesthetic terms. That [Donald] Trump's plugs on *The Apprentice* simply lack finesse. That, compared to say E.T.'s Reese's Pieces, a product that received an 80 percent boom after it was in [Steven] Spielberg's movie, the CoverGirl banter on *America's Next Top Model* is just plain awkward. Product placement done well can add realism to a scene—it might seem strange if Tony Soprano [character from *The Sopranos*] were drinking no-name soda rather than Coke [Coca-Cola]—whereas product integration usually makes the entire show seem fake.

"Trusted" and "Important"

But let's now go back to the words "trusted" and "important." Not in reference to the Dallas disc jockeys or Jeff Probst [host of *Survivor*] or any of the other hosts who shill with such skill, but in respect to the other "trusted" and "important" sources that have given them such a pass. When KZPS made its late April [2007] announcement, there wasn't much fuss. Most articles tempered the news by mentioning it had been unsuccessfully tried by three Long Island [New York] stations before. Some even likened the Clear Channel move to the kind of sponsorship used in public radio, noting that Kelly Kibler, the sales director behind the Dallas station format change, used to work for NPR's [National Public Radio's] *Car Talk*.

A Fallacious Claim

The argument that product placements add realism is suspect. Products that are placed in entertainment vehicles, are, almost without exception, positively cast. A reality that shows the branded portion of our world in unyielding positive light is a false one. To only "name names" when the angel's halo appears above is disingenuous. We know from our experience with cigarette brands, automobile brands, fast-food brands, and the like that brands do not necessarily correlate with health, safety, or happiness. So to say that product placements enhance reality is necessarily a fallacious claim. It is akin to saying that television commercials reflect reality. What is reflected is of course a highly selective vision of the world that is in the best interests of the sponsoring party. While product placements may not be so forthright, there are laws to protect people from deceptive practices in advertising, while product placement largely passes under the radar screen.

Lawrence A. Wenner,
"On the Ethics of Product Placement in Media Entertainment,"
in Handbook of Product Placement in the Mass Media:
New Strategies in Marketing Theory, Practice, Trends,
and Ethics, *ed. Mary-Lou Galician. New York: Routledge, 2004.*

But having a sponsor and chatting up about said sponsor are fundamentally different. Even if the hosts, like *Car Talk*'s Tom [Magliozzi] and Ray [Magliozzi] who, unlike most NPR shows, announce the underwriters themselves, they don't go as far as to say they both have Allstate Insurance and, boy, they sure as heck feel like they are in good hands. Their shameless commerce division is still pretty divided. By paralleling the two stations, mainstream media reduces Clear

Channel's move to more of the same. It permits that this latest version of branded content is inevitable and insures similar corporate ventures go even less noticed.

After all, once something "just is," it's easy for us to forget it could be any other way. As with reality television, the more pervasive this sort of integration becomes, the less press it gets, the more normal it seems, the less critical we media consumers become.

This wasn't the case. In 2005, the Writers Guild of America and the Screen Actors Guild staged a protest, urging a "code of conduct" on the use of product integration in TV. Among their demands for a limit of product placement in children's advertising, they also called for "full and clear disclosure for both the visual and aural disclosure of product integration deals at the beginning of each program so the program's audience knows ahead of time that it will be subject to hidden or stealth advertising." The FCC [Federal Communications Commission], however, decided it was much ado about nothing, and the story quickly slipped off the news cycle.

As with integration, decrying the media's short attention span seems like a futile fight. Except that it's a story the media might be less and less tempted to return to. It's hard, after all, for the Philly *Inquirer* to protest branded content when its business section is being visibly funded by Citizens Bank. CBS's *60 Minutes* might hesitate after Philips sponsored one of its episodes; or any other media outlet faced with online and cable competition when it realizes how much it can make if it gets into the game itself. Spending on product placement alone is projected to top 3.7 billion in America this year [2007]. So Clear Channel keeps shilling. Sitcom story lines increasingly involve products. The plugs grow more aggressive. The ads creep on.

But here is also where it gets interesting. The Internet and cable, so often fingered as reasons why product integration has become necessary, are also providing some interesting advertising alternatives. Because as old media looks at ways of disbanding traditional ads, new media is increasingly fitting them in. Most news Web sites preface their videos with short, separate and clearly defined commercials. YouTube recently announced that, starting next year, it will begin playing pre-roll ads to most of their videos. Qtrax, a music-sharing site, is offering free music as long as one watches a short commercial first. A broadcasting executive has been floating the idea of a pay-per-system cable: The more ads you watch, the lower your bill.

Subverting Choice

Granted, a lot of cable today is as product-plugged as the main networks. And obviously, with blogs-for-hire and corporately produced viral videos, the Internet is hardly immune to stealth advertising. But what's important to note here is that opposed to mainstream media, a lot of these new media advertising models emphasize consumer awareness. If you want the video, the music or the show for free, you accept the commercial fee. If you prefer not to be exposed to the sales pitch, you pay for Sirius or HBO or a Web site's premium membership. It may come with a cost, but at least the choice is yours.

The changing media landscape begs many questions: questions about consumer choice and corporate disclosure; questions that in the best circumstances leave it to viewers to decide the cost/benefit ratio of our advertising consumption and that, in the worst, subvert any choice we have at all.

Unfortunately, these are not questions mainstream media is likely to ask. A call against advertising creep is often marginalized as extreme or anti-American. But the opposite of product integration is not communism, it's consent. And if we can't always have the freedom of such choice, it's important that as media consumers, we at least force the conversation.

Periodical Bibliography

The following articles have been selected to supplement the diverse views presented in this chapter.

Eric Clemons — "Why Advertising Is Failing on the Internet," *TechCrunch*, March 22, 2009.

Tom Lowry — "Pandora: Unleashing Mobile Phone Ads," *BusinessWeek*, May 21, 2009.

Andrew Adam Newman — "The Body as Billboard: Your Ad Here," *New York Times*, February 17, 2009.

J. Scott Orr — "Advertisers Flocking to the Internet, Where the (Inter)action Is," *Star-Ledger* (New Jersey), February 3, 2008.

Gina Piccalo — "Beach Break," *Los Angeles* (magazine), August 2008.

Joel Rubinson — "Seven Predictions About the Future of Advertising," *Fast Company*, June 16, 2009.

Tom Walton — "Blatant or Blurred, Product Placement Is Intrusive," *Blade* (Toledo, Ohio), June 22, 2009.

Jennifer Wells — "Advertising's Holy Grail," *Globe and Mail* (United Kingdom), March 14, 2008.

Robin Wight, as told to Jo Adetunji — "It's the Future of Advertising, of Everything," *Guardian* (United Kingdom), February 23, 2009.

Troy Young — "It's Time to Get Back to Basics," *Adweek*, March 10, 2009.

For Further Discussion

Chapter 1

1. Lucas Conley contends that as advertising becomes more sophisticated, it erodes the public's trust. Do you agree or disagree with the author? Cite from the texts to explain your response.

2. Joy Parks writes that many sexist advertisements of the mid-twentieth century have been created by women and for women. In your opinion, was this a form of female empowerment? Why or why not?

3. Richard Westlund states that cause marketing benefits social causes. Anne Kingston, on the other hand, alleges that cause marketing can undermine a cause because it encourages consumerism, not activism. In your opinion, who makes the stronger argument? Why or why not?

Chapter 2

1. Karen Sternheimer claims that fears about youth and advertising underestimate what children know and how they think. Does Diane E. Levin take children's emotional and intellectual abilities for granted? Use examples from the viewpoints to support your answer.

2. David Jernigan and Trevor Butterworth and Rebecca Goldin, PhD, maintain, in different ways, that alcohol ads in magazines do not target children. While they have different views on alcohol advertising and youth, do the authors' similar claims confuse the reader? Why or why not?

Chapter 3

1. June Kronholz argues that attack ads are not effective. David Mark disagrees, however, saying that attack ads provide vital information about candidates and the issues. Whose position is more persuasive? Cite examples from the texts to explain your response.

2. Marj Halperin advocates free airtime for political candidates. Would this requirement, as Bob Priddy asserts, restrict networks' and broadcasters' editorial decisions? Use examples from the viewpoints to support your answer.

Chapter 4

1. Douglas Haddow claims that Burger King's Facebook campaign signals the end of advertising. Considering her support for Web advertising, how would Alison Overholt view Burger King's Internet marketing strategy? Explain your answer.

2. Brian Stelter and Alicia Rebensdorf agree that today's product placements resemble corporate sponsorships of variety shows and soap operas of the past. In your opinion, is this a positive or negative trend? Why or why not?

Organizations to Contact

The editors have compiled the following list of organizations concerned with the issues debated in this book. The descriptions are derived from materials provided by the organizations. All have publications or information available for interested readers. The list was compiled on the date of publication of the present volume; the information provided here may change. Be aware that many organizations take several weeks or longer to respond to inquiries, so allow as much time as possible.

Ad Council
815 Second Avenue, 9th Floor, New York, NY   10017
(212) 922-1500
e-mail: info@adcouncil.org
Web site: www.adcouncil.org

Ad Council is a nonprofit organization that works with businesses, advertisers, the media, and other nonprofit groups to produce and distribute public service campaigns. It also conducts research to improve the effectiveness of its campaigns. Several research studies can be found on its Web site.

Adbusters Media Foundation
1243 West Seventh Avenue, Vancouver, BC   V6H 1B7
  Canada
(604) 736-9401 • fax: (604) 737-6021
e-mail: info@adbusters.org
Web site: www.adbusters.org

Adbusters Media Foundation is a network of artists, activists, writers, and others who strive to build a new social activist movement. The organization publishes *Adbusters* magazine, which explores the ways that commercialism destroys physical and cultural environments. Spoof ads and information on political action are available on its Web site.

Advertising Standards Canada (ASC)
175 Bloor Street E, South Tower, Suite 1801
Toronto, ON   M4W 3R8
  Canada
(416) 961-6311 • fax: (416) 961-7904
e-mail: info@adstandards.com
Web site: www.adstandards.com

Advertising Standards Canada (ASC) is an organization with more than 160 corporate members, including advertising agencies and the media. It promotes the use of industry self-regulation as a way to ensure the integrity of advertising. The Canadian Code of Advertising Standards and links to advertising industry associations and self-regulatory bodies can be found on its Web site.

Association of National Advertisers (ANA)
708 Third Avenue, 33rd Floor, New York, NY   10017
(212) 697-5950 • fax: (212) 687-7310
Web site: www.ana.net

Association of National Advertisers (ANA) is a trade association that offers resources and training to the advertising industry. Its members provide services and products to more than three hundred companies that combined spend more than $100 billion on advertising and marketing. The association publishes *Advertiser* magazine six times each year and other publications are available on its Web site.

The Campaign Legal Center (CLC)
215 E Street NE, Washington, DC   20002
(202) 736-2200 • fax: (202) 736-2222
e-mail: info@campaignlegalcenter.org
Web site: www.campaignlegalcenter.org

The Campaign Legal Center (CLC) is a nonprofit, nonpartisan organization that represents the public in campaign finance issues and associated media laws. The center also develops legal and policy debate on political advertising. Its Web site features articles and weekly reports.

Center for a New American Dream

6930 Carroll Avenue, Suite 900, Takoma Park, MD   20912
(301) 891-3683
e-mail: newdream@newdream.org
Web site: www.newdream.org

The Center for a New American Dream's goal is to help Americans consume responsibly and thus protect the earth's resources and improve the quality of life. Its Kids and Commercialism Campaign provides information on the effects of advertising on children. The center publishes booklets and newsletters.

Children's Advertising Review Unit (CARU)

70 West Thirty-sixth Street, 12th Floor, New York, NY   10018
(866) 334-6272
e-mail: caru@caru.bbb.org
Web site: www.caru.org

As the children's branch of the U.S. advertising industry's self-regulation program, Children's Advertising Review Unit (CARU) reviews ads aimed at children and promotes responsible children's advertising. It also corrects misleading or inaccurate commercials with the help of advertisers. Commentary and articles are available on its Web site.

Commercial Alert

PO Box 19002, Washington, DC   20036
(202) 387-8030 • fax: (202) 234-5176
Web site: www.commercialalert.org

Commercial Alert is a nonprofit organization with the goal of preventing commercial culture from exploiting children and destroying family and community values. It works toward that goal by conducting campaigns against commercialism in classrooms and marketing to children. News and opportunities to take action against various marketing tactics are posted on its Web site.

Federal Trade Commission (FTC)
Bureau of Consumer Protection
600 Pennsylvania Avenue NW, Washington, DC   20580
(877) 382-4357 (FTC-HELP)
Web site: www.ftc.gov/bcp/

Part of the Federal Trade Commission (FTC), the Bureau of Consumer Protection defends consumers against fraudulent or destructive practices. The bureau's Division of Advertising Practices protects people from deceptive advertising by monitoring advertisements for numerous products, including tobacco, alcohol, and over-the-counter (OTC) drugs.

Interactive Advertising Bureau (IAB)
116 East Twenty-seventh Street, 7th Floor
New York, NY   10016
(212) 380-4700
Web site: www.iab.net

More than 375 leading media and technology companies who are responsible for selling 86 percent of online advertising in the United States comprise the Interactive Advertising Bureau (IAB). On behalf of its members, the IAB is dedicated to the growth of the interactive advertising marketplace, of its share of total marketing spend, and of its members' share of total marketing spend. The IAB educates marketers, agencies, media companies, and the business community about the value of interactive advertising. Working with its member companies, the bureau evaluates and recommends standards and practices and fields critical research on interactive advertising.

Media Awareness Network
1500 Merivale Road, 3rd Floor, Ottawa, ON   K2E 6Z5
   Canada
(613) 224-7721 • fax: (613) 224-1958
e-mail: info@media-awareness.ca
Web site: www.media-awareness.ca

Media Awareness Network is a nonprofit organization that promotes media education and develops media literacy programs. The Media Issues section of its Web site examines topics such as marketing to children and stereotyping in advertisements. Its Web site also contains information for parents and educators.

MediaChannel

575 Eighth Avenue, New York, NY   10018
(212) 246-0202 • fax: (212) 246-2677
e-mail: david@mediachannel.org
Web site: http://mediachannel.org

MediaChannel is a nonprofit Web site that explores global media issues. In addition to news, commentaries, reports, and discussion forums, the site also provides articles about political advertising, marketing to children, and the advertising industry.

Bibliography of Books

Allen P. Adamson   *BrandSimple: How the Best Brands Keep It Simple and Succeed.* New York: Palgrave Macmillan, 2006.

Joel Bakan   *The Corporation: The Pathological Pursuit of Profit and Power.* New York: Free Press, 2004.

Marcel Danesi   *Why It Sells: Decoding the Meanings of Brand Names, Logos, Ads, and Other Marketing and Advertising Ploys.* Lanham, MD: Rowman & Littlefield, 2008.

Scott Donaton   *Madison & Vine: Why the Entertainment and Advertising Industries Must Converge to Survive.* New York: McGraw-Hill, 2004.

John Grant   *The Green Marketing Manifesto.* Hoboken, NJ: Wiley & Sons, 2007.

Tom Himpe   *Advertising Is Dead! Long Live Advertising!* London, UK: Thames & Hudson, 2006.

Naomi Klein   *No Logo: No Space, No Choice, No Jobs.* New York: Picador, 2000.

Martin Lindstrom   *Buyology: Truth and Lies About Why We Buy.* New York: Broadway Business, 2008.

Gavin Lucas and Michael Dorrian   *Guerrilla Advertising: Unconventional Brand Communication.* London, UK: Lawrence King Publishers, 2006.

David Mark — *Going Dirty: The Art of Negative Campaigning.* Lanham, MD: Rowman & Littlefield, 2009.

Carrie McLaren and Jason Torchinsky, eds. — *Ad Nauseam: A Survivor's Guide to American Consumer Culture.* New York: Faber & Faber, 2009.

Kenneth Roman — *The King of Madison Avenue: David Ogilvy and the Making of Modern Advertising.* New York: Palgrave Macmillan, 2009.

John Samples — *The Fallacy of Campaign Finance Reform.* Chicago, IL: University of Chicago Press, 2006.

Karen Sternheimer — *Connecting Social Problems and Popular Culture: Why the Media Is Not the Problem.* Boulder, CO: Westview Press, 2009.

Max Sutherland — *Advertising and the Mind of the Consumer: What Works, What Doesn't, and Why.* Sydney, NSW, Australia: Allen & Unwin, 2009.

Mark Tungate — *Ad Land: A Global History of Advertising.* London, UK: Kogan, 2007.

David Vinjamuri — *Accidental Branding: How Ordinary People Build Extraordinary Brands.* Hoboken, NJ: John Wiley & Sons, 2008.

Christopher Vollmer and Geoffrey Precourt

Always On: Advertising, Marketing, and Media in an Era of Consumer Control. New York: McGraw-Hill, 2008.

Darrell M. West

Air Wars: Television Advertising in Election Campaigns, 1958–2008. Washington, DC: CQ Press, 2009.

Index